This book is dedicated to the intrepid adventurers and explorers of the digital age, who brave the unknown territories of artificial intelligence with curiosity and courage. May your quest for knowledge illuminate the path forward for all of humanity.

The Future of AI and Society

By Alan Ingles

Preface

At the heart of the twenty-first century's technological renaissance lies a concept both profoundly transformative and deeply enigmatic: Artificial Intelligence (AI). This term, once relegated to the realms of science fiction and speculative thought, has rapidly evolved to become a cornerstone of contemporary society. AI's ascent from a niche interest to a global powerhouse reflects not just an advancement in technology but a fundamental shift in how we envision the future of humanity. This book, "The Future of AI and Society," aims to demystify AI, tracing its journey from theoretical roots to its current status as a driver of change, while exploring the implications of this evolution for jobs, ethics, and human interactions.

AI, in its broadest definition, refers to machines or systems capable of performing tasks that typically require human intelligence. These tasks range from recognizing speech, making decisions, translating languages, to identifying patterns. The journey of AI begins in the mid-20th century, born out of the quest to understand if machines could think. From the creation of simple algorithms to the development of neural networks that mimic the human brain, AI has grown in complexity and capability.

The evolution of AI can be segmented into waves, each marked by significant breakthroughs and shifts in understanding. The first wave in the 1950s and 60s saw the birth of AI as an academic discipline, where the focus was on problem-solving and symbolic methods. The second wave, starting in the 1980s, was fueled by improvements in machine learning and neural networks, leading to systems capable of learning from data. We are currently riding the crest of AI's third wave, characterized by AI's ubiquity and the integration of AI into everyday life. This era is defined by big data, advanced algorithms, and the increasing synergy between AI and other technologies like blockchain and the Internet of Things (IoT).

The current state of AI technology is both impressive and daunting. AI systems can now defeat human champions in complex games, drive cars, create art, write texts, and diagnose diseases, often surpassing human performance in specific tasks. These advancements raise profound questions about the role of AI in our future, its impact on employment, ethics, privacy, and the essence of human-machine interaction.

This book seeks to navigate the intricate landscape of AI's impact on society. Its purpose is twofold: firstly, to provide a comprehensive understanding of how AI technologies came to be and where they are headed; and secondly, to critically examine the implications of these technologies on various facets of human life. Through a balanced discourse, "The Future of AI and Society" aims to equip readers with the knowledge to participate in shaping a future where AI and humanity coexist beneficially.

The scope of this book encompasses a wide range of topics, including but not limited to, the transformation of the job market due to automation, ethical considerations in AI development, the changing nature of human interactions influenced by AI, and the societal challenges and opportunities that AI presents. By examining both the positive potential and the risks associated with AI, this book intends to foster a nuanced understanding of this complex field.

I look forward to you joining me in this journey of discovery.

Alan Ingles

Chapter 1 – The AI Revolution

The narrative of AI is a fascinating journey through time, marked by human curiosity, ingenuity, and an unyielding drive to breach the unknown. This chapter unfolds the tapestry of AI's evolution, spotlighting key milestones and the profound societal impacts they've ignited. As we traverse from the inception of AI to the cutting-edge technologies shaping today's revolution, we uncover a story not just of machines and algorithms but of a paradigm shift in human history.

A Brief History of AI Development

The genesis of AI can be traced back to the ancient myths of intelligent robots and artificial beings, which reflect humanity's perennial fascination with creating life-like intelligence. However, the scientific pursuit of AI began much later, in the mid-20th century. The 1950s heralded the formal birth of AI as an academic discipline, when the term "Artificial Intelligence" was first coined at the Dartmouth Conference in 1956. This period saw the development of foundational algorithms and the proposal of the Turing Test by Alan Turing, a method to evaluate a machine's ability to exhibit intelligent behavior indistinguishable from that of a human.

The early years of AI were marked by optimism and bold predictions. Pioneers like Marvin Minsky and John McCarthy believed that creating a thinking machine was just a matter of time and the right algorithm. The 1960s and 70s saw significant advancements with the creation of ELIZA, a natural language processing computer program, and SHRDLU, a program capable of answering questions about objects in a virtual world. However, the initial enthusiasm met with technical limitations, leading to the first of several "AI winters," a period of reduced funding and interest in AI research due to unmet expectations.

The 1980s brought a resurgence of interest in AI, spurred by the development of expert systems, which were programs designed to mimic the decision-making abilities of a human expert in specific domains. This period also saw the introduction of machine learning, a subset of AI that enables machines to learn from data, improving their performance over time without being explicitly programmed.

Milestones in AI and Their Societal Impact

Each milestone in AI's development has left an indelible mark on society. The introduction of IBM's Deep Blue, which defeated world chess champion Garry Kasparov in 1997, shattered the long-held belief that certain intellectual tasks were beyond the capability of machines. This event not only showcased the potential of AI in problem-solving and strategic planning but also prompted a societal reckoning with the capabilities and future role of intelligent machines.

The 21st century witnessed an explosion of AI applications, driven by advances in machine learning and the availability of big data. In 2011, IBM's Watson won the quiz show "Jeopardy!," competing against two of the show's greatest champions. This demonstrated AI's ability to understand complex language, process vast amounts of information, and deliver precise answers in real-time, foreshadowing its potential in fields like customer service, education, and healthcare.

Another landmark achievement was the development of AlphaGo by DeepMind, which defeated the world champion in Go, a game known for its deep strategic complexity, in 2016. This victory was significant because it highlighted the power of deep learning and neural networks, techniques that allow AI to learn and improve from experience, akin to human learning.

These milestones have had profound societal impacts, challenging our understanding of intelligence and creativity. They have sparked debates on the ethical implications of AI, the future of work, and the potential need for new governance and regulatory frameworks. Furthermore, they've catalyzed the integration of AI into various sectors, revolutionizing industries and creating new opportunities for innovation and efficiency.

Current Technologies Driving the AI Revolution

The AI revolution is being fueled by several key technologies, each contributing to the rapid advancement and adoption of AI across different spheres of society.

Machine Learning and Deep Learning: At the heart of the AI revolution is machine learning, particularly deep learning, which utilizes neural networks with many layers to learn complex patterns in large amounts of data. These technologies have been pivotal in advancing natural language processing, computer vision, and predictive analytics.

Cloud Computing: The accessibility of cloud computing has democratized AI, enabling startups and large enterprises alike to harness powerful computing resources. This has accelerated the development and deployment of AI models, fostering innovation and scalability.

Big Data: The exponential growth in data generation has provided the fuel for AI's advancement. Big data technologies enable the collection, storage, and analysis of vast datasets, facilitating more sophisticated and accurate AI models.

IoT: IoT has expanded the frontier for AI applications, with interconnected devices providing real-time data that AI systems can analyze and act upon. This integration has led to advancements in smart homes, autonomous vehicles, and intelligent industrial systems.

Quantum Computing: Though still in its infancy, quantum computing represents a future leap in processing power, with the potential to solve complex problems beyond the reach of current AI technologies. Quantum computing promises to dramatically accelerate the capabilities of AI, enabling the processing of vast datasets in fractions of a second and potentially unlocking new algorithms that could redefine what AI can achieve. This fusion of quantum computing and AI holds the promise of significant advancements in drug discovery, climate modeling, and complex system simulation, offering solutions to some of the world's most pressing challenges.

The Interplay of AI with Emerging Technologies

The AI revolution is not occurring in isolation but in tandem with the maturation of other emerging technologies, creating a synergistic effect that amplifies the transformative potential of each.

Blockchain: The integration of AI with blockchain technology offers new ways to secure AI-driven transactions, protect data privacy through decentralized networks, and create transparent, unalterable records of AI decisions. This combination could revolutionize industries requiring high levels of trust and security, such as finance, healthcare, and supply chain management.

Augmented Reality (AR) and Virtual Reality (VR): AI enhances AR and VR experiences by enabling more interactive and personalized content. In education, for example, AI-driven AR and VR can create immersive learning experiences tailored to individual learning styles and needs. In entertainment, AI can generate dynamic, responsive environments, transforming how we engage with digital content.

Edge Computing: As AI applications become more integrated into daily life, the need for real-time processing grows. Edge computing, where data processing occurs on the device itself rather than in a distant data center, enables faster responses by AI systems in applications such as autonomous vehicles and real-time health monitoring devices. AI algorithms optimized for edge computing can operate with lower latency and reduced bandwidth, making smart technology more efficient and accessible.

Societal Impact of Current AI Technologies

The current wave of AI technologies is having a profound impact on society, reshaping industries, influencing job markets, and prompting ethical and philosophical debates.

Industry Transformation: AI is revolutionizing sectors from manufacturing to healthcare, introducing efficiencies and capabilities previously unimaginable. In manufacturing, AI-driven predictive maintenance can prevent downtime, saving companies millions. In healthcare, AI algorithms can diagnose diseases from images with accuracy surpassing human experts, potentially democratizing access to high-quality medical diagnostics.

Job Market Evolution: The automation of routine tasks by AI is shifting the landscape of work, creating a demand for new skills and roles. While some jobs are being rendered obsolete, AI is also generating opportunities for employment in tech-driven sectors and necessitating a re-skilling of the workforce to adapt to the new digital economy.

Ethical and Privacy Concerns: The pervasive use of AI raises significant ethical questions, particularly regarding data privacy, surveillance, and the potential for algorithmic bias. As AI systems become more integral to decision-making processes, ensuring these systems are transparent, fair, and accountable becomes crucial.

Human-AI Interaction: AI is changing the nature of human interaction, not only with technology but also with each other. From social media algorithms influencing our perceptions to chatbots providing company, AI is redefining human relationships, posing questions about the nature of connection and community in an increasingly digital world.

Conclusion

The AI revolution is reshaping the fabric of society, propelled by advancements in machine learning, quantum computing, and the synergistic integration with other emerging technologies. As we stand at the precipice of this new era, the promise of AI is immense, offering solutions to some of humanity's most intractable problems. However, this revolution also demands careful navigation, with concerted efforts to address the ethical, social, and economic challenges it presents.

The future of AI and its impact on society will be shaped by the decisions we make today—how we choose to develop, regulate, and integrate these technologies into our lives. As we move forward, it is imperative that we do so with a mindful approach, ensuring that the AI revolution leads to a future where technology enhances human well-being, fosters equity, and respects our shared values.

Chapter 2 – AI in the Workplace

The dawn of AI and automation heralds a transformative era for the global job market. As these technologies continue to evolve, their integration into various industries is not only reshaping the landscape of work but also challenging our conventional understanding of employment. This chapter delves into the intricate dynamics of automation and AI's impact across different sectors, highlighting both the challenges and opportunities they present for the workforce. Through detailed case studies, we explore real-world examples of AI integration in the workplace, ultimately uncovering the nuanced potential for job creation in the AI era.

Automation and the Future of Jobs

The discourse surrounding automation and the future of jobs is often painted with a broad brush of optimism or doom. On one hand, the fear of job displacement looms large, with predictions of widespread unemployment as machines and algorithms assume tasks historically performed by humans. On the other hand, a more hopeful perspective suggests that automation could free humans from mundane tasks, paving the way for more creative and fulfilling work.

The reality, however, lies in the complexity of transition. Automation, driven by advancements in AI, is poised to redefine roles rather than simply erase them. The key to navigating this transition is adaptability. The workforce of the future will need to harness new skills, pivot into emerging sectors, and embrace lifelong learning to stay abreast of technological advancements.

AI's Impact on Various Industries

The integration of AI and automation into various industries is creating a tapestry of change, characterized by both disruption and development.

Manufacturing: AI-driven automation in manufacturing has led to increased efficiency, safety, and quality control. Robots equipped with AI algorithms can perform repetitive tasks with precision, operate in hazardous environments, and adapt to new production lines with minimal intervention. While this shift has streamlined operations, it also necessitates a workforce skilled in robotics, AI maintenance, and digital management.

Healthcare: The healthcare sector has witnessed a remarkable infusion of AI, from diagnostic algorithms and robotic surgery to personalized medicine and patient care automation. AI tools are enhancing the accuracy of diagnoses, optimizing treatment plans, and revolutionizing patient monitoring. These advancements are not replacing medical professionals but augmenting their capabilities, requiring new competencies in digital health technologies and data analysis.

Finance: In finance, AI is reshaping everything from customer service to fraud detection and investment strategies. Chatbots and virtual assistants, powered by AI, are improving customer experiences, while algorithms analyze vast datasets to identify fraudulent activity or optimize portfolios. This transformation is creating demand for professionals skilled in AI, data science, and cybersecurity, alongside traditional financial expertise.

Case Studies of AI Integration in the Workplace

Case Study 1: Automotive Manufacturing: A leading automotive manufacturer implemented AI-driven robots for assembly line tasks traditionally done by humans, such as welding and part installation. This shift resulted in a 20% increase in production efficiency and a significant reduction in workplace injuries. To support this transition, the company launched a reskilling initiative, offering employees training in robot operation, AI system maintenance, and digital quality control.

Case Study 2: Telemedicine Service: A telehealth provider introduced an AI-powered diagnostic tool that assists doctors in analyzing symptoms and medical images. This tool has expanded access to healthcare, especially in remote areas, and allowed doctors to focus on patient care rather than administrative tasks. The platform's success has spurred job growth in IT support, digital healthcare consultancy, and remote patient monitoring services.

Case Study 3: Financial Advisory Firm: An investment firm integrated AI algorithms to tailor investment advice based on real-time market analysis and individual client profiles. This personalized approach has improved client satisfaction and investment outcomes. The firm has since expanded its workforce, hiring data scientists, AI developers, and financial analysts skilled in interpreting AI-generated insights.

Potential for Job Creation in the AI Era

The narrative that AI and automation will lead to mass unemployment overlooks the potential for job creation inherent in technological advancement. As AI reshapes industries, it also spawns new sectors and roles. The demand for AI specialists, data scientists, and cybersecurity experts is on the rise, alongside jobs in AI ethics, policy, and regulation.

Moreover, AI and automation are catalyzing innovation, leading to the emergence of startups and businesses focused on AI applications, from environmental sustainability to healthcare solutions. These ventures not only contribute to economic growth but also create diverse employment opportunities.

The transition to an AI-driven economy also highlights the importance of soft skills, such as creativity, emotional intelligence, and problem-solving. As machines take on routine tasks, human-centric skills become more valuable, emphasizing the role of education and training in preparing the workforce for the future.

The integration of AI and automation into the workplace presents a dual narrative of challenge and opportunity. While the displacement of certain jobs is inevitable, the overall impact of AI on the job market is not a zero-sum game. The future of work in the AI era will be characterized by transformation rather than diminution, with new roles emerging as rapidly as old ones evolve or become obsolete. This dynamic landscape demands a proactive approach to workforce development, emphasizing the importance of reskilling and continuous learning.

The potential for job creation in the AI era extends beyond merely replacing lost jobs; it offers the opportunity to elevate the quality of work and life. For instance, AI-driven innovations can lead to more meaningful employment, where human intelligence and creativity are leveraged for tasks that machines cannot replicate, such as empathetic interaction, complex decision-making, and creative endeavors. Moreover, the augmentation of jobs with AI can enhance productivity and job satisfaction, by relieving employees from mundane tasks and enabling them to focus on more strategic and fulfilling aspects of their work.

Governments, educational institutions, and businesses play crucial roles in facilitating this transition. Policy frameworks need to be developed to support workforce retraining programs, encourage lifelong learning, and ensure equitable access to education and digital resources. Similarly, organizations must invest in training and development programs to equip their employees with the skills needed for an AI-driven future. Educational institutions, on their part, should adapt curricula to include AI literacy, data science, and critical thinking, preparing students not just for the jobs of today but for the evolving landscape of tomorrow.

The integration of AI in the workplace also calls for a re-evaluation of social contracts and labor laws to address the challenges posed by gig economy jobs, which are likely to increase as AI and automation reshape traditional employment models. Issues such as job security, income stability, and access to benefits need to be addressed to ensure a fair and inclusive transition to the future of work.

Embracing a New Paradigm

As we stand on the cusp of a new era in the world of work, the narrative around AI and jobs is shifting from one of displacement to empowerment. The focus is increasingly on how AI can augment human capabilities and foster an environment where humans and machines collaborate to achieve outcomes that were previously unimaginable.

This collaborative future requires an openness to change, a commitment to lifelong learning, and a proactive approach to personal and professional development. It also calls for a collective effort from all sectors of society to ensure that the benefits of AI are distributed equitably, and that no one is left behind in this technological leap forward.

The stories of AI integration in manufacturing, healthcare, finance, and other industries serve as testament to the transformative power of AI. These case studies not only showcase the efficiencies and innovations brought about by AI but also highlight the resilience and adaptability of the human spirit. They underscore the fact that the future of work is not something to be feared but embraced, with the potential to usher in an era of unprecedented growth, creativity, and fulfillment.

Conclusion

The AI era is not a distant future; it is unfolding here and now, reshaping the landscape of work in profound ways. The journey ahead is fraught with challenges but also brimming with opportunities. By embracing change, fostering a culture of lifelong learning, and prioritizing human-centric skills, we can navigate the transition to an AI-augmented workplace with optimism and purpose.

Ultimately, the future of work in the AI era is a blank canvas, with the potential to redefine what it means to work, create, and contribute to society. As we chart our course through this uncharted territory, the guiding principle should be clear: to leverage AI not as a substitute for human capabilities but as a complement to them, enhancing our creativity, empathy, and ingenuity. In doing so, we can forge a future where technology and humanity coalesce to create a more prosperous, equitable, and fulfilling world.

Chapter 3 – Ethical Considerations in AI

As AI weaves itself into the fabric of society, it brings to the fore a complex array of ethical considerations. The rapid advancement and integration of AI technologies in various facets of life present not just opportunities for progress but also significant moral dilemmas. This chapter delves into the ethical quandaries posed by AI, exploring issues of bias, fairness, privacy, and the development of guidelines for ethical AI. Through a comprehensive examination, we aim to shed light on the path towards a more equitable and responsible AI future.

Moral Dilemmas Posed by AI Technologies

The deployment of AI technologies introduces a spectrum of moral dilemmas, challenging our traditional ethical frameworks. One of the most illustrative examples of these ethical quandaries is the adaptation of the classic "trolley problem" to the context of autonomous vehicles. This thought experiment asks whether an AI-controlled car, faced with an unavoidable accident, should prioritize the safety of its passengers or the lives of pedestrians. The decision becomes even more complex when the variables increase: What if the pedestrians are jaywalking, or if sacrificing the passenger could save more lives? This scenario not only highlights the need for sophisticated moral decision-making frameworks within AI systems but also emphasizes the critical importance of these systems' ability to evaluate and act upon ethical dilemmas in real-time. The consequences of these decisions are far-reaching, potentially affecting the trust in and societal acceptance of autonomous technologies.

Expanding upon these concerns, another significant ethical dilemma arises from the deployment of AI in decision-making systems across various sectors, including law enforcement, financial lending, and employment. These systems are engineered to enhance efficiency, reduce human error, and provide objective assessments. However, the reality is often far from objective. For instance, AI systems used in predictive policing can inadvertently lead to over-policing in marginalized communities if the data fed into them reflects historical biases. Similarly, AI-driven lending algorithms might deny loans to individuals based on zip codes or other proxies for race or economic status, perpetuating systemic inequalities. In the realm of hiring, AI can favor candidates based on criteria that reflect past hiring biases, such as attending certain universities or possessing characteristics that are irrelevant to job performance but reflect societal prejudices.

These instances underscore a critical ethical tension: the promise of AI to deliver fairness and efficiency is in constant negotiation with the risk of entrenching existing societal biases. The question, then, is not merely technical but profoundly ethical: How can we ensure that AI systems promote social justice and equity? Addressing this requires a multi-faceted approach. First, it necessitates the development and implementation of algorithms that are not only technically proficient but also socially aware, capable of identifying and mitigating biases in their decision-making processes. This involves a critical examination of the data sets on which these algorithms are trained, ensuring they are representative and free from historical biases.

Moreover, the challenge extends beyond the technical realm into the regulatory and philosophical. There needs to be a robust ethical framework guiding the deployment of AI in sensitive areas, encompassing principles of fairness, accountability, and transparency. Regulators and policymakers must play a critical role in establishing standards and guidelines that ensure AI systems are developed and used in ways that do not perpetuate discrimination but rather advance the cause of social equity. This requires an interdisciplinary approach, bringing together experts from technology, ethics, sociology, and law to collaboratively tackle these challenges.

Additionally, the development of AI systems must be democratized, involving stakeholders from diverse backgrounds in the design, development, and deployment processes. This participatory approach can help ensure that a wide range of perspectives and values are considered, making the systems more robust, equitable, and aligned with societal norms and expectations.

The ethical dilemmas presented by the deployment of AI technologies are profound and multifaceted, touching on deep philosophical questions about morality, justice, and human rights. Navigating these dilemmas requires more than technological prowess; it demands a concerted effort from technologists, ethicists, policymakers, and society at large to develop AI systems that are not only intelligent and efficient but also fair, transparent, and aligned with the broader values of society. By addressing these ethical challenges head-on, we can harness the transformative power of AI to create a future that respects and enhances human dignity and equity.

Bias and Fairness in Machine Learning Algorithms

Bias and fairness in machine learning algorithms are critical issues that underscore the complexities of ethical AI development. The essence of bias in AI systems stems from the data on which these systems are trained. Machine learning, the technological heart of many AI applications, operates by discerning patterns within datasets to make predictions or decisions. However, if these datasets carry the imprint of historical biases or fail to accurately represent the full spectrum of human diversity, the resulting AI systems inadvertently perpetuate these biases. This phenomenon is not merely theoretical; it has manifested in various real-world applications, leading to discriminatory outcomes. For instance, facial recognition technologies have been documented to exhibit lower accuracy rates for women and people of color, raising significant concerns about the fairness and reliability of these systems. Similarly, AI-driven recruitment tools have demonstrated a tendency to favor candidates based on gender or ethnicity, mirroring and amplifying societal biases present in the training data.

The challenge of bias in AI is emblematic of the broader ethical considerations in technology development. It reflects the ways in which societal inequalities can be embedded and exacerbated by technological systems, leading to outcomes that reinforce existing disparities. This situation calls for a rigorous and comprehensive approach to address bias and promote fairness in AI. Ensuring fairness in AI is not a one-time fix but a continuous process that requires diligence and commitment throughout the entire lifecycle of AI development.

Firstly, diversifying the datasets used for training AI systems is a fundamental step. This involves not only including a wide range of demographic characteristics but also ensuring that the data captures a breadth of experiences, perspectives, and contexts. Diverse datasets can help mitigate the risk of overlooking important variables or perpetuating stereotypes, leading to more accurate and equitable AI systems.

Secondly, the development of algorithms capable of identifying and correcting for bias is paramount. This technical challenge requires innovative approaches to algorithm design, such as the incorporation of fairness constraints or the use of techniques that can adjust biased data distributions. By embedding mechanisms for bias detection and correction directly into the algorithms, developers can create AI systems that are more reflective of ethical principles and societal values.

Moreover, incorporating fairness as a core metric in the evaluation of AI systems is essential. This entails developing robust metrics and benchmarks that can assess the fairness of AI outputs across different groups and scenarios. By holding AI systems to rigorous standards of fairness, stakeholders can ensure that these technologies contribute positively to society and do not inadvertently harm vulnerable populations.

Additionally, addressing bias and ensuring fairness in AI necessitates the involvement of diverse teams in the development process. Diversity in AI development teams is not merely a matter of representation; it is a crucial factor in building AI systems that are sensitive to a wide array of human experiences and perspectives. Diverse teams bring a multiplicity of viewpoints to the table, enabling the identification and mitigation of potential biases that may not be apparent to a more homogenous group. This diversity extends beyond demographic factors to include interdisciplinary expertise, ensuring that ethical, social, and cultural considerations are integrated into the design and implementation of AI systems.

Addressing bias and ensuring fairness in AI is a multifaceted challenge that requires a concerted effort across technical, procedural, and organizational dimensions. By diversifying datasets, developing algorithms that can detect and correct bias, incorporating fairness as a key evaluation metric, and fostering diverse development teams, stakeholders can work towards creating AI systems that are equitable, reliable, and aligned with societal values. The commitment to fairness in AI is not just a technical necessity but a moral imperative, reflecting the collective responsibility to harness the power of AI in ways that uplift and empower all members of society.

Privacy Concerns with AI Applications

In the digital era, the proliferation of AI technologies has elevated privacy to a critical area of concern. The inherent capabilities of AI to gather, scrutinize, and take action based on extensive data collections bring forth profound implications for individual rights and societal norms concerning privacy, autonomy, and consent. The issue is particularly acute in scenarios where AI systems, under the guise of efficiency and personalization, might compromise personal privacy. For example, surveillance applications powered by AI have the potential to infringe upon individual privacy, conducting monitoring and tracking operations that individuals may not be aware of, much less consent to. This not only raises ethical alarms but also legal and social concerns about the extent to which technology should penetrate private lives.

Similarly, in sectors such as healthcare and finance, AI-driven services offer unparalleled personalization, deriving insights from deeply personal data to provide tailored advice, diagnoses, or financial products. While these services can significantly benefit individuals by offering more accurate, timely, and relevant services, they simultaneously pose a risk of exposing sensitive personal information. The disclosure of such information, whether inadvertently or through security breaches, can have lasting repercussions on an individual's privacy and, by extension, their autonomy and dignity.

Addressing these privacy concerns necessitates a comprehensive and proactive approach, underpinned by robust data protection frameworks and the incorporation of privacy-by-design principles in the development and deployment of AI systems. Privacy-by-design is a concept that advocates for privacy to be considered throughout the engineering process of AI systems, ensuring that privacy safeguards are baked into the technology from the ground up rather than being tacked on as an afterthought. This approach entails the adoption of stringent data handling and processing practices that prioritize data minimization, ensuring that only the data necessary for a specific purpose is collected and retained.

Furthermore, ensuring transparency in AI operations is crucial for maintaining public trust and accountability. Individuals should be informed about how their data is being used, the purposes of data processing, and the measures in place to protect their privacy. This transparency is not only about compliance with legal standards but also about empowering individuals with the knowledge and tools they need to control their personal information.

Giving individuals control over their data is another cornerstone of navigating privacy concerns in AI. This involves implementing mechanisms that allow users to access their data, correct inaccuracies, and, where appropriate, delete their information. Such controls empower individuals, giving them a say in how their data is used and ensuring that their participation in AI-driven services is based on informed consent.

In addition to these foundational principles, the development and adoption of privacy-preserving AI technologies offer promising paths for balancing the benefits of AI with the imperative to protect individual privacy. Technologies like federated learning, which enables AI models to be trained across multiple decentralized devices or servers without exchanging the data itself, and differential privacy, which adds randomness to datasets to prevent the identification of individuals, are examples of innovative approaches to safeguarding personal information. These technologies allow for the utilization of AI's analytical capabilities while minimizing the risk of compromising personal privacy.

In conclusion, as AI continues to integrate into every facet of our lives, addressing the privacy concerns it engenders is paramount. Through a combination of robust legal frameworks, ethical considerations, technological innovations, and a commitment to transparency and individual control, it is possible to harness the immense potential of AI while respecting and protecting the privacy of individuals. This balanced approach is essential for ensuring that AI serves as a tool for enhancing human life, grounded in respect for individual rights and societal values.

Guidelines and Frameworks for Ethical AI

The creation of ethical AI systems is a complex, multifaceted challenge that requires the cooperation and collective wisdom of a broad spectrum of stakeholders. This collaboration spans disciplines, including technology, law, philosophy, and social sciences, acknowledging that the ethical implications of AI transcend any single field. The goal is to create AI that serves humanity positively, respecting fundamental human rights and promoting a fair and equitable society. Recognizing this, numerous organizations, academic institutions, and governments worldwide have embarked on the ambitious task of developing comprehensive guidelines and frameworks to guide the ethical development, deployment, and governance of AI technologies. These guidelines represent a consensus on core ethical principles that should underpin AI systems, including transparency, accountability, fairness, and respect for human rights.

For example, the European Union (EU) has been at the forefront of this effort with its Ethics Guidelines for Trustworthy AI. The guidelines articulate seven key requirements that AI systems should meet to be deemed ethical. These include ensuring human oversight to keep human judgment at the center of AI decisions; fostering diversity and non-discrimination to prevent AI from perpetuating societal biases; and prioritizing societal and environmental well-being to ensure AI contributes positively to societal challenges and respects ecological limitations. Another notable initiative is the IEEE Global Initiative on Ethics of Autonomous and Intelligent Systems, which provides a detailed set of standards designed to promote ethically aligned design principles in the development of AI and autonomous systems. These standards cover a broad range of ethical considerations, from ensuring the protection of personal data to fostering AI systems that are transparent and understandable by their human users.

The practical implementation of these guidelines necessitates a deep integration of ethical considerations into the AI development lifecycle. This means not only adhering to ethical principles during the design and deployment of AI systems but also continuously monitoring and assessing these systems once they are in use. Conducting ethical impact assessments becomes a critical tool in this process, enabling developers and policymakers to identify potential ethical risks and societal impacts of AI technologies before they are fully deployed. Such assessments can help in the formulation of strategies to mitigate negative impacts, ensuring that AI technologies contribute to the common good.

Engaging with a diverse array of stakeholders is another vital aspect of implementing ethical AI guidelines. This engagement should include not only AI developers and ethicists but also representatives from vulnerable communities, policymakers, and the general public. By understanding the potential societal impacts of AI from a broad range of perspectives, developers can create more inclusive, equitable AI systems. Furthermore, this engagement can help identify emerging ethical issues as AI technologies evolve, ensuring that ethical guidelines remain relevant over time.

Establishing governance structures is also crucial for the ethical implementation of AI. These structures should provide clear mechanisms for accountability, ensuring that AI developers and users are responsible for the outcomes of AI systems. This includes establishing clear lines of responsibility for AI-induced harms and setting up redressal mechanisms for those adversely affected by AI decisions. Such governance structures should be transparent and accessible, enabling effective oversight of AI technologies and fostering trust among the public.

The development of ethical AI is an ongoing, collaborative endeavor that requires continuous effort and vigilance. The guidelines and frameworks proposed by various entities offer a solid foundation for ethical AI, but their effectiveness depends on their practical implementation. By embedding ethical considerations into every stage of AI development, engaging with diverse stakeholders, and establishing robust governance structures, we can ensure that AI technologies are developed and deployed in ways that respect human rights, promote fairness, and contribute positively to society. This collaborative approach to ethical AI not only mitigates the risks associated with AI technologies but also maximizes their potential to serve as a force for good in the world.

Conclusion

The ethical considerations in AI present a complex landscape that requires careful navigation. As AI technologies become increasingly embedded in our lives, the imperative to address moral dilemmas, bias, privacy concerns, and the development of ethical frameworks becomes ever more pressing. Achieving ethical AI necessitates a collaborative effort, involving policymakers, technologists, ethicists, and the broader public in an ongoing dialogue.

The path towards ethical AI is not straightforward, fraught with challenges and uncertainties. However, by fostering an environment of transparency, inclusivity, and accountability, we can harness the transformative potential of AI while safeguarding fundamental ethical values. The journey towards ethical AI is a collective one, requiring a commitment to continuous learning, adaptation, and vigilance. As we navigate this moral maze, our guiding light must be the unwavering pursuit of an AI future that enhances human dignity.

Chapter 4 – AI and Human Interaction

The advent of AI has not only revolutionized industries but has also profoundly transformed the nature of human interaction. From altering the fabric of communication to introducing AI in personal relationships and blending the digital with the physical, AI's influence is pervasive. This chapter delves into these aspects, exploring how AI shapes our interactions and the psychological effects of these evolving dynamics.

How AI is Changing the Way We Communicate

AI technologies have dramatically reshaped how we interact and communicate in our increasingly digital world. This transformation is not just superficial; it goes deep into the fabric of daily human interaction, changing not only the methods but also the pace and accessibility of communication. AI-powered chatbots and virtual assistants, now common across various platforms, serve as the first point of contact in customer service interactions, capable of handling an extensive range of inquiries with remarkable speed and efficiency. These systems, through their ability to process and analyze vast amounts of data, offer responses that are not only immediate but also increasingly personalized. They take into account the user's past interactions, preferences, and even sentiment, to tailor their responses in a way that feels engaging and human-like. This level of personalization significantly enhances the user experience, making digital interactions more intuitive and satisfying.

Beyond providing answers and assistance, AI systems have revolutionized the way we manage our daily lives. They help organize schedules, set reminders, make recommendations, and even manage other smart devices within our homes, becoming an integral part of the personal organization and lifestyle management. This seamless integration of AI into personal life speaks to a broader trend of digital assistants becoming more like companions, blurring the lines between tool and collaborator.

AI's impact on breaking down language barriers represents another monumental shift in global communication. AI-driven translation and transcription services enable real-time, accurate translations, allowing people from different linguistic backgrounds to engage in meaningful conversations without the need for human translators. This capability has profound implications for global business, education, and social interactions, enabling more inclusive and diverse conversations than ever before. The ability to communicate across language barriers with ease fosters a greater sense of global community and understanding, making information and dialogue accessible to a wider audience.

Furthermore, AI's role in content creation has opened new avenues for disseminating information and storytelling. Algorithms capable of generating news articles, marketing materials, and creative content are not only speeding up content creation processes but also challenging our notions of creativity and authorship. These AI-driven content creation tools can analyze trends, adapt to stylistic nuances, and produce content that resonates with specific audiences, enhancing both the relevance and reach of digital content.

This capability is particularly transformative for the media and marketing industries, where the demand for fresh, personalized content is ever-growing.

However, the proliferation of AI in communication also raises important questions about authenticity, privacy, and the potential loss of human touch in interactions. As AI systems become more sophisticated and embedded in our communication networks, ensuring these technologies augment rather than replace human connection becomes crucial.

In conclusion, AI technologies have fundamentally changed the landscape of communication, introducing efficiencies and capabilities that were once unimaginable. From enhancing customer service with chatbots and virtual assistants to breaking down language barriers and revolutionizing content creation, AI has made communication more accessible, personalized, and efficient. As we navigate this new digital communication era, the challenge will be to leverage these advancements in a way that enriches human interaction without sacrificing the personal touch and authenticity that define meaningful communication.

AI in Personal Relationships: Assistance and Companionship

The sophistication of AI technologies has ushered in a new era for personal relationships, extending the realm of AI's influence to include not just task-oriented assistance but also elements of emotional support and companionship. The proliferation of virtual assistants, embedded in a myriad of devices from smartphones to smart home systems, marks a significant evolution in our interaction with technology. These AI entities, programmed to perform a variety of tasks such as managing schedules, setting reminders, and offering personalized advice, have become integral to daily life for many. Their ability to process and respond to user inputs in a manner that simulates human interaction has led to an intriguing phenomenon where users begin to view these virtual assistants not just as tools, but as companions. This anthropomorphizing of AI systems reflects a deeper psychological inclination to seek connection and understanding, even from artificial entities.

Beyond the functional convenience they offer, virtual assistants have started playing a role akin to that of a personal confidant or advisor for some users. By analyzing user preferences, behaviors, and even vocal intonations, these AI systems can offer tailored advice, from culinary recommendations to workout suggestions, simulating a level of personal insight traditionally reserved for close human relationships. This growing intimacy with AI has sparked discussions around the nature of companionship and the human need for interaction, pushing the boundaries of how personal relationships are defined.

In parallel, the development of more advanced AI companions designed explicitly for emotional support represents a significant leap toward fulfilling human social and emotional needs through technology. These AI companions are equipped with sophisticated algorithms enabling them to engage in meaningful conversations, recognize emotional cues, and adapt their responses to the user's mood and context. Unlike traditional virtual assistants focused on task management, these AI entities aim to provide a deeper level of emotional engagement, offering comfort, encouragement, and a semblance of understanding. For individuals facing loneliness, social anxiety, or simply seeking additional emotional support, AI companions present a novel avenue for connection.

However, the integration of AI into personal relationships is not without its complexities and ethical considerations. As users form attachments to these AI companions, questions arise about the nature of the connections formed and their impact on human emotional health. The interaction with AI companions, while providing immediate comfort and a sense of being understood, also blurs the lines between artificial and genuine human connections. This dynamic introduces a nuanced landscape of emotional interaction, where the benefits of companionship must be weighed against the potential for isolation or the diminishing value placed on human-to-human relationships.

Furthermore, the reliance on AI for emotional support raises questions about privacy, data security, and the potential for manipulation. As AI systems learn from interactions to provide more personalized responses, they accumulate sensitive personal information, necessitating robust safeguards to protect user privacy and ensure ethical use of data.

The expanding role of AI in personal relationships reflects a transformative shift in the interaction between humans and technology. The emergence of AI companions capable of providing both assistance and emotional support has the potential to enrich lives, offering new forms of companionship and redefining the essence of connection. However, navigating this new terrain requires careful consideration of the ethical, psychological, and social implications, ensuring that as we embrace the possibilities of AI, we remain attentive to the fundamental human values that underpin meaningful personal relationships.

The Blending of Digital and Physical Worlds Through AI

AI has been instrumental in blurring the lines between the digital and physical realms, facilitating a seamless integration of both worlds that has dramatically transformed our daily lives and interactions with our environment. Through the advent of AR and VR, AI has unlocked new dimensions of experience, enabling a fusion of digital information with the tangible world around us. These immersive technologies, fueled by AI's processing power, are capable of rendering complex, interactive environments that respond to user inputs in real-time, offering experiences that range from enhanced reality to completely virtual worlds.

In the entertainment industry, AI-driven AR and VR have revolutionized gaming, introducing a level of immersion and interactivity previously unattainable. Players can now enter and interact with 3D worlds that feel real, engaging in experiences that extend beyond the screen into the physical space around them. Beyond entertainment, education has been transformed by these technologies, with AI creating dynamic, interactive learning environments that engage students in a more profound and impactful manner. Virtual labs, historical recreations, and 3D models offer hands-on learning without the physical constraints, enabling students to explore complex concepts in a safe and controlled environment.

Healthcare is another sector witnessing a transformative impact from the integration of AI, AR, and VR. Remote medical consultations, powered by AI, have become more effective, with physicians able to assess and diagnose conditions as if they were physically present with the patient. Moreover, AR and VR applications, guided by AI, are being used for surgical training, patient rehabilitation, and therapy, providing realistic simulations and environments that enhance both learning and healing processes.

Parallel to these developments, the IoT stands as a testament to the profound integration of AI into our physical spaces. Smart homes and cities, empowered by AI, have gone beyond mere convenience, evolving into ecosystems that intelligently adapt to and anticipate the needs of their inhabitants. In these interconnected environments, devices do not operate in isolation; instead, they communicate with each other and the broader network, making decisions to optimize for comfort, energy efficiency, and security. This orchestration, managed by AI, transforms living and communal spaces into intelligent environments that reflect the preferences and requirements of their users, from adjusting lighting and temperature to enhancing security measures and managing energy consumption efficiently.

The integration of AI into physical spaces also extends to urban planning and environmental management, where AI-enabled systems analyze vast amounts of data to optimize traffic flow, public transportation, and energy usage. These smart cities represent a forward-thinking approach to addressing contemporary challenges, such as congestion, pollution, and resource management, showcasing the potential of AI to not only enhance individual lives but also improve societal well-being.

As AI continues to weave the digital and physical worlds closer together, the potential for creating spaces that truly respond to and enhance human interaction grows. This convergence promises a future where our environments, augmented by digital information and powered by AI, become more responsive and attuned to our needs, embodying a level of interactivity and personalization that enriches the human experience. However, as we navigate this integrated future, the importance of maintaining ethical standards, privacy, and security remains paramount, ensuring that the blending of digital and physical worlds through AI enhances rather than detracts from the quality of human life.

The Psychological Effects of AI Interactions

The psychological effects of engaging with AI technologies are complex and varied, encompassing a broad spectrum of impacts on human behavior, cognition, and emotional states. As AI becomes more embedded in daily life, offering both practical assistance and forms of companionship, it brings about significant changes in how individuals perceive and interact with the world around them.

On the positive side, AI systems designed to provide assistance in daily tasks or companionship have shown potential to mitigate feelings of isolation or loneliness for many individuals. The constant availability of these AI systems, something no human counterpart could sustain, offers a sense of presence and interaction that can be comforting to those who might otherwise feel disconnected. By taking over mundane or routine tasks, these AI technologies can also lessen the cognitive burden on individuals. This reduction in mental load can lead to lower levels of stress and anxiety, as people find themselves with more time and energy to devote to activities that are meaningful and fulfilling, potentially enhancing overall life satisfaction.

Moreover, AI-driven tools and platforms can support mental health by offering therapeutic interventions, mood tracking, and personalized mental health advice. These applications can make mental health support more accessible, providing users with resources that they might not have sought out in traditional settings due to stigma, financial constraints, or accessibility issues.

However, the proliferation of AI in personal and social contexts also introduces several concerns regarding psychological well-being and the nature of human relationships. The ease and convenience of interacting with AI, while beneficial in many respects, may inadvertently lead to a decrease in human-to-human interactions. Overreliance on digital companionship could impede the development of critical social skills and emotional intelligence, particularly in younger individuals who are still forming these abilities. This shift towards digital forms of interaction might result in a diminished capacity for empathy, problem-solving, and navigating complex emotional landscapes in real-life settings.

The omnipresence of AI in communication channels also presents challenges related to information overload, privacy, and data security. Constant notifications, recommendations, and digital interactions can overwhelm individuals, leading to difficulty concentrating, heightened anxiety, and a sense of being perpetually tethered to digital devices. Privacy concerns arise as AI systems require access to personal data to function optimally, making users vulnerable to breaches and unauthorized data use, further exacerbating feelings of anxiety and mistrust.

The convergence of digital and physical realities through AI-enhanced technologies like augmented reality (AR) and virtual reality (VR) adds another layer to the psychological impact of AI. While these technologies offer innovative ways to enhance educational content, entertainment, and social interactions, they also blur the lines between digital and physical experiences. This blurring can alter perceptions of reality, potentially impacting how individuals engage with the physical world and each other. The long-term effects on cognitive processes, such as attention, memory, and spatial awareness, as well as on social behaviors and relationships, remain areas of active investigation and concern.

In summary, the psychological effects of AI interactions encapsulate a dichotomy of potential benefits and challenges. While AI can offer valuable support, companionship, and efficiency, leading to positive outcomes for mental health and well-being, it also poses risks related to social skills development, privacy, and the nature of human experience. Navigating this complex landscape requires a balanced approach, emphasizing the development and use of AI in ways that enhance human capabilities and enrich lives, while also being mindful of the need to maintain meaningful human connections and protect individual privacy and security. As we forge ahead into an increasingly AI-integrated future, it becomes crucial to continue exploring these psychological impacts, ensuring that technology serves to support and enhance human well-being, rather than detract from it.

Conclusion

The intersection of AI and human interaction is transforming the way we communicate, relate, and perceive the world around us. As AI becomes increasingly embedded in our daily lives, it is essential to critically examine the implications of these technologies on human behavior, relationships, and psychological well-being. By navigating the challenges and embracing the opportunities presented by AI, we can leverage these technologies to enhance human interaction, while remaining mindful of the importance of preserving the human elements of connection, empathy, and emotional depth. As we move forward, the ongoing dialogue between technology and humanity will shape the future of AI in human interaction, striving for a balance that augments the human experience without diminishing the value of genuine human connections.

Chapter 5 – AI in Governance and Surveillance

The integration of AI into governance and surveillance has opened up new frontiers in public administration, policy-making, and security. While AI offers the promise of enhanced efficiency, transparency, and safety, it also raises significant ethical questions and concerns about privacy and civil liberties. This chapter explores the multifaceted role of AI in governance and surveillance, the delicate balance between safety and privacy, and the overarching ethical considerations that must guide the responsible use of AI in these domains.

AI's Role in Public Administration and Policy Making

The utilization of AI in public administration and policy-making marks a significant evolution in governance, heralding a new era where decision-making processes are increasingly driven by data and technology. This paradigm shift offers the potential to not only enhance the efficiency of government operations but also to elevate the level of service provided to citizens. AI's ability to digest and interpret vast datasets allows for a level of analysis and foresight previously unattainable, promising to revolutionize various aspects of public administration.

One of the key areas where AI is making a substantial impact is in the optimization of public services. By automating routine tasks, AI systems free up valuable time for public servants, allowing them to focus on more complex and nuanced aspects of governance. Moreover, AI-driven platforms can facilitate more effective communication between governments and citizens, providing timely updates on services, processing inquiries and feedback, and tailoring communication to individual needs. This not only improves the responsiveness of public services but also enhances transparency and trust in governmental processes.

Additionally, AI technologies are instrumental in the predictive maintenance of public infrastructure. By analyzing data from sensors and other sources, AI algorithms can identify patterns and predict potential system failures in everything from transportation networks to water supply systems. This predictive capability enables governments to undertake maintenance and repairs proactively, avoiding costly breakdowns and ensuring the continuous delivery of essential services. Such pre-emptive action not only conserves public funds but also minimizes inconvenience to citizens, contributing to higher standards of living and public satisfaction.

In the sphere of policy-making, AI's capacity to process and analyze extensive datasets offers a transformative approach to understanding and addressing societal challenges. By leveraging AI for data analysis, policymakers can gain deep insights into the dynamics of complex issues such as urban growth, social inequality, and environmental sustainability. This data-driven approach allows for the development of more nuanced and effective policies that are tailored to the specific conditions and needs of the population. For instance, AI models that simulate the socioeconomic impacts of different policy scenarios can provide policymakers with a clear understanding of the potential benefits and drawbacks of their decisions, facilitating more informed and strategic policy development.

Furthermore, AI technologies play a crucial role in enhancing the evidence base for policy-making. Through the collection and analysis of data on policy implementation and outcomes, AI systems can help evaluate the effectiveness of public policies and programs. This enables a continuous feedback loop where policies are adjusted and refined based on empirical evidence of what works. Such an approach to policy-making not only increases the likelihood of achieving desired outcomes but also fosters a culture of accountability and continuous improvement in public administration.

The integration of AI into public administration and policy-making presents unparalleled opportunities for enhancing governmental efficiency, responsiveness, and effectiveness. By harnessing the power of AI for data analysis, predictive maintenance, and evidence-based policy-making, governments can better serve the needs of their citizens and address complex societal challenges. However, the successful implementation of AI in governance requires careful consideration of ethical, privacy, and security concerns to ensure that the benefits of technology are realized in a manner that respects the rights and freedoms of individuals. As we move forward, the role of AI in public administration and policy-making is set to become increasingly central, heralding a future where governance is characterized by greater efficiency, transparency, and responsiveness to the needs of society.

Surveillance, Security, and AI: Balancing Safety and Privacy

The integration of AI into the domains of surveillance and security has seen a meteoric rise, revolutionizing the way monitoring and safety operations are conducted. This surge is largely attributed to significant leaps in machine learning algorithms, facial recognition technologies, and predictive analytics, all of which have expanded the capabilities of surveillance systems beyond traditional methods. Today, AI-driven surveillance tools are extensively applied in a variety of settings, including but not limited to public areas, transportation hubs, border control, and digital platforms, significantly augmenting the capacity to detect and thwart potential security threats and criminal activities.

AI's prowess in analyzing real-time video feeds enables security systems to detect anomalies, recognize faces with astonishing accuracy, and even predict potential incidents before they occur. For example, sophisticated AI systems can sift through hours of video footage to pinpoint unusual patterns or behaviors that may indicate a security threat, such as unattended baggage at an airport or an individual repeatedly scouting a sensitive location. This level of surveillance, powered by AI, extends to the digital realm where algorithms monitor online behavior and communications to identify and mitigate cyber threats, fraud, and other illicit activities, thereby safeguarding national security and public welfare.

Moreover, the advent of AI in security practices has facilitated the development of smart border control solutions, where biometric data and facial recognition technologies expedite the identification process, enhancing both efficiency and security. Similarly, in the context of public safety, AI-enabled systems are deployed to manage crowd control, monitor traffic flow, and ensure the smooth conduct of large public events, thereby pre-empting situations that could potentially escalate into safety hazards.

Despite the undeniable benefits AI brings to surveillance and security, its widespread adoption has ignited a fervent debate over privacy implications and the risk of governmental overreach. The ability of AI systems to conduct surveillance unobtrusively and gather comprehensive data on individuals raises profound concerns regarding privacy invasion and the ethical use of technology. The constant accumulation and analysis of personal information by AI, often without explicit consent or awareness of the individuals involved, challenge the foundational principles of privacy and civil liberties.

This scenario necessitates the establishment of stringent legal and regulatory frameworks that govern the use of AI in surveillance. There is a pressing need for policies that strike an equitable balance between leveraging AI for public safety and safeguarding individual rights to privacy. Such frameworks should mandate transparency in the operation of AI surveillance systems, specify the scope and limitations of surveillance activities, and ensure that data collection practices adhere to principles of necessity and proportionality.

Additionally, mechanisms for accountability and oversight are crucial to prevent misuse and abuse of AI surveillance technologies. Independent audits, public oversight bodies, and the provision of recourse for individuals affected by AI-driven surveillance are essential components of a robust governance structure. These measures not only protect against the potential excesses of surveillance but also build public trust in the use of AI for security purposes.

In conclusion, while AI presents unparalleled opportunities for enhancing surveillance and security operations, its application must be navigated with a careful consideration of ethical implications and privacy concerns. The development of comprehensive legal frameworks, coupled with strict oversight mechanisms, is imperative to ensure that the deployment of AI in surveillance strikes the right balance between advancing public safety and protecting individual freedoms. As we move forward, the challenge lies in harnessing the benefits of AI-enhanced surveillance in a manner that respects and upholds the principles of democracy and human rights.

Ethical Considerations and Civil Liberties

The ethical landscape of employing AI within the realms of governance and surveillance is intricate, raising profound questions about fairness, justice, and the preservation of civil liberties in the digital age. As governments and institutions increasingly rely on AI to enhance decision-making processes, monitor public spaces, and implement policies, the imperative to address the ethical implications of these technologies becomes paramount.

Bias in AI systems is a critical issue that threatens to perpetuate and even amplify existing inequalities. Given that AI algorithms learn from historical data, there is a substantial risk that these systems will inherit and perpetuate the biases present in the data they are fed. This can result in unfair treatment of certain groups within law enforcement practices, where predictive policing tools may disproportionately target specific communities, or within public service delivery, where algorithms might inadvertently prioritize or disadvantage individuals based on biased criteria. The challenge extends to policy-making, where AI-driven insights could skew towards outcomes that do not equitably serve the whole population. Ensuring the transparency of AI algorithms is a necessary step toward accountability, allowing for scrutiny and understanding of how decisions are made. However, transparency alone is insufficient without mechanisms to ensure that these systems are held accountable for their impact on individuals and communities. It is vital that AI systems not only operate in ways that are understandable but that there are also clear avenues for redress when injustices occur.

Moreover, the ethical implications of AI in governance and surveillance deeply intersect with fundamental human rights and civil liberties, such as the freedoms of expression and association, and particularly the right to privacy. The deployment of AI technologies for purposes such as mass surveillance and data collection presents a tangible threat to the privacy of individuals, enabling unprecedented levels of monitoring and data analysis by governments and other actors. This capability, if left unchecked, could be utilized to suppress dissent, censor free speech, or infringe upon the right to privacy, under the guise of national security or public order. The potential misuse of AI in these contexts underscores the urgent need for a governance framework that places human rights and ethical principles at the forefront of technology deployment.

In addressing these challenges, a principled approach rooted in the respect for human rights and civil liberties is essential. This approach demands more than passive adherence to ethical norms; it requires active engagement with the public, stakeholders, and affected communities to ensure that the deployment of AI technologies aligns with societal values and democratic principles. Public engagement fosters a sense of shared responsibility and trust, providing valuable insights that can guide the ethical development and application of AI. Moreover, it emphasizes the necessity of building AI systems that not only respect but also enhance civil liberties and democratic values.

Furthermore, safeguarding democratic values in the age of AI necessitates robust legal and regulatory frameworks that explicitly address the ethical challenges posed by AI in governance and surveillance. These frameworks should provide clear guidelines on the permissible uses of AI, establish standards for transparency and accountability, and ensure that individuals have the means to challenge and seek redress for decisions made by or with the assistance of AI. Ensuring that AI serves the public good, rather than undermining it, requires a commitment to ongoing ethical reflection, regulatory oversight, and the willingness to adapt policies as our understanding of these technologies and their impact evolves.

In sum, the ethical considerations surrounding AI in governance and surveillance demand a comprehensive and nuanced response that balances the benefits of these technologies with the imperative to protect individual rights and maintain the fabric of democratic society. By committing to transparency, accountability, public engagement, and the respect for civil liberties, policymakers and technologists can navigate the ethical complexities of AI, ensuring that these powerful tools enhance, rather than erode, the principles of fairness, justice, and democracy.

Conclusion

AI's integration into governance and surveillance presents a dual-edged sword, offering significant opportunities to enhance public administration, safety, and security, while also posing challenges to privacy, ethics, and civil liberties. Navigating this landscape requires a careful and principled approach, underpinned by strong regulatory frameworks, ethical guidelines, and a commitment to protecting the rights and freedoms of individuals. As we continue to explore the potentials of AI in these critical areas, the focus must remain on harnessing the benefits of technology in a way that upholds democratic values, fosters trust, and ensures the well-being of citizens in the digital age.

Chapter 6 – The Global AI Landscape

The rapid advancements in AI technology have not been confined to any single geography or nation; it is a global phenomenon with widespread implications for international relations, economic development, and global governance. Countries around the world are adopting and regulating AI in diverse ways, leading to a complex tapestry of AI development that reflects varying national priorities, ethical considerations, and economic ambitions. This chapter explores the multifaceted nature of the global AI landscape, examining how different nations are approaching AI, the role of international collaborations and competitions, and the geopolitical implications of AI advancements.

How Different Countries are Adopting and Regulating AI

The adoption and regulation of AI across the globe present a kaleidoscope of strategies, shaped by distinct cultural, economic, and political landscapes. This diversity reflects the multifaceted nature of AI itself, capable of being harnessed for a wide array of purposes, from enhancing economic efficiency to addressing societal challenges and reshaping the military landscape.

In the United States, the approach to AI has been characterized by a dynamic and robust ecosystem driven primarily by the private sector. Companies like Google, Amazon, and Microsoft have not only been at the forefront of AI research and development but have also been instrumental in applying AI across various sectors, including healthcare, finance, and retail. The U.S. government's regulatory stance has been relatively hands-off, opting for a policy framework that fosters innovation and growth within the AI sector while starting to confront critical issues such as privacy, algorithmic bias, and the implications of AI on national security. This approach aims to maintain the United States' position as a leader in technological innovation while addressing the ethical and societal impacts of AI deployment.

China's strategy, on the other hand, illustrates a comprehensive state-driven approach to AI development. With the government's active involvement, China has rapidly emerged as a formidable player in the global AI arena. The "New Generation Artificial Intelligence Development Plan" is a testament to China's ambition to dominate the AI landscape by 2030, highlighting the strategic importance of AI across various sectors, including defense, economy, and social governance. This centralized strategy not only aims to propel China to the forefront of AI technology but also to integrate AI as a pivotal element in enhancing governmental efficiency and societal management.

The European Union offers a contrasting model, prioritizing ethical considerations and the safeguarding of fundamental human rights in the development and application of AI. The EU's comprehensive regulatory framework, including the GDPR, serves as a benchmark for privacy and data protection, reflecting a commitment to developing AI technologies that are trustworthy, transparent, and aligned with democratic values. This approach seeks to balance innovation with ethical considerations, ensuring that AI serves the public interest and contributes to societal well-being.

Emerging economies such as India and Singapore are also embracing AI, viewing it as a catalyst for social and economic transformation. India's approach to AI, for instance, emphasizes solving societal challenges such as healthcare accessibility and agricultural productivity, leveraging AI to enhance the quality of life for its vast population. Similarly, Singapore's strategic deployment of AI in public services and urban management exemplifies how AI can be utilized to streamline governmental operations and improve citizen engagement. These countries demonstrate the potential of AI to drive sustainable growth and address pressing societal needs, underscoring the role of AI in supporting development agendas.

Moreover, countries like Japan and South Korea have adopted unique approaches that blend technological innovation with societal needs. Japan's focus on leveraging AI to address demographic challenges, such as an aging population, showcases the potential of AI in healthcare and eldercare. South Korea's investment in AI education and research highlights the importance of fostering a knowledge economy that can support continuous innovation in AI.

This global panorama of AI adoption and regulation illustrates the vast potential of AI to shape societies, economies, and international relations. However, it also underscores the need for global dialogue and cooperation to address the challenges posed by AI, including ethical dilemmas, privacy concerns, and the digital divide. As nations continue to navigate the complex landscape of AI, the diversity of approaches offers valuable lessons on harnessing AI for the benefit of humanity while safeguarding against its potential risks.

International Collaborations and Competitions in AI Development

The international dimension of AI development is marked by an intricate web of collaborations and competitions that span the globe, highlighting the dual nature of cooperation and rivalry that underpins the advancement of this transformative technology. These international efforts are pivotal in shaping the trajectory of AI research, innovation, and application, fostering an environment where knowledge and expertise are shared freely across borders, and where challenges are addressed through collective wisdom.

At the heart of these global interactions are multinational research initiatives that bring together the brightest minds from various countries to work on cutting-edge AI projects. These collaborations often result in groundbreaking discoveries that propel the field forward, demonstrating the power of collective effort over solitary endeavor. Furthermore, cross-border partnerships between academic institutions and corporations play a crucial role in translating academic research into practical applications. Such collaborations not only accelerate the pace of AI development but also ensure that innovations are disseminated widely, benefiting a larger segment of the global population.

Global AI conferences and symposiums serve as melting pots of ideas and innovation, where researchers, practitioners, and policymakers from around the world converge to discuss the latest trends, challenges, and opportunities in AI. These gatherings are instrumental in fostering a sense of community among AI enthusiasts and professionals, encouraging the exchange of ideas and facilitating collaborations that might not have been possible within the confines of national borders.

Competitions in AI, such as the International Conference on Learning Representations (ICLR) and the Neural Information Processing Systems (NeurIPS), play a crucial role in driving innovation and excellence in the field. By challenging participants to develop solutions to complex problems, these competitions not only advance the state of the art in AI but also serve as platforms for emerging talent to gain recognition and for established researchers to benchmark their work against global standards. The competitive spirit of these events, coupled with the opportunity for learning and networking, makes them vital components of the global AI ecosystem.

However, the spirit of competition extends beyond academic and technical challenges, reflecting broader geopolitical and economic ambitions. Nations around the world recognize the strategic value of AI as a driver of economic growth, national security, and global influence. This has led to a scenario where countries are not only collaborating on AI research and development but are also competing to establish dominance in the AI arena. This competition manifests in increased government funding for AI initiatives, strategic partnerships between states and corporations, and policies aimed at attracting and retaining AI talent. The race for AI supremacy is reshaping international relations, with AI emerging as a key factor in economic and diplomatic negotiations.

This complex landscape of international collaborations and competitions in AI underscores the multifaceted nature of global AI development. While competition spurs nations to invest in AI research and innovation, fostering economic and strategic advantages, collaboration remains essential for addressing the ethical, social, and technical challenges posed by AI. Balancing these dynamics is crucial for ensuring that AI development is guided by a shared vision that benefits humanity as a whole. As the global community navigates this delicate balance, the future of AI will likely be characterized by both increased cooperation and intensified competition, with profound implications for the advancement of technology and the shaping of the international order.

The Geopolitical Implications of AI Advancements

The rapid advancements in AI technology have ushered in a new era in the global geopolitical landscape. Nations across the world are increasingly recognizing the strategic value of AI, not just as a tool for economic growth but also as a critical component of national security and defense strategies. This recognition has spurred a competitive drive among countries to achieve AI supremacy, which, while fostering innovation and technological advancement, also harbors the potential for escalating international tensions and rivalries.

AI's role in enhancing the capabilities of military and intelligence operations is a significant factor contributing to the notion of an AI arms race. Countries are investing heavily in AI to develop advanced surveillance systems, autonomous weapons, and cyber defense mechanisms. These investments are driven by the belief that AI will be central to future warfare and intelligence strategies, offering significant advantages in terms of speed, precision, and efficiency. However, the militarization of AI raises ethical concerns and poses the risk of sparking an arms race, as nations seek to outpace each other in developing AI technologies that could alter the balance of power on the global stage.

The challenge of establishing a cohesive global governance framework for AI further complicates the geopolitical implications of AI advancements. The absence of an international consensus on how AI should be developed, regulated, and used makes it difficult to align the diverse approaches and interests of different countries. This lack of uniformity not only hampers efforts to set global standards for ethical AI development but also impedes the creation of mechanisms to ensure that the benefits of AI are distributed equitably across nations. The disparity in AI capabilities and access between developed and developing countries could widen existing socioeconomic gaps, underscoring the need for international cooperation and dialogue to address these disparities.

Moreover, the impact of AI on the global economy and labor markets is profound and far-reaching. The automation of tasks across various sectors, driven by AI, is reshaping the nature of work and the skills required in the workforce. While AI has the potential to boost productivity and create new types of jobs, it also poses the risk of significant job displacement, affecting income distribution and social stability. The transition to an AI-driven economy could exacerbate income inequality both within countries and on a global scale, as nations with advanced AI capabilities reap disproportionate benefits, leaving others behind.

This economic transformation has implications for international trade as well. AI-driven innovations could alter trade dynamics by changing the comparative advantages of countries and reshaping global supply chains. Nations that excel in AI technology could dominate new markets, potentially leading to trade imbalances and friction. As such, the global spread of AI technology necessitates thoughtful policy responses to manage its economic effects, ensure fair competition, and support workers displaced by automation.

In summary, the geopolitical landscape of AI is marked by both opportunities and challenges. The race for AI dominance underscores the technology's strategic importance, but it also highlights the need for global cooperation to manage the risks associated with AI militarization and to bridge the divide between AI leaders and laggards. Establishing global norms for AI governance and ensuring that AI advancements lead to inclusive and equitable benefits require concerted effort and dialogue among the international community. As nations navigate the complexities of the AI era, fostering collaboration and addressing the socioeconomic implications of AI will be crucial for maintaining global stability and promoting shared prosperity.

Conclusion

The global AI landscape is a complex and dynamic domain, shaped by diverse national strategies, international

collaborations, and geopolitical considerations. As countries around the world navigate the opportunities and challenges presented by AI, the need for thoughtful regulation, ethical guidance, and international cooperation becomes increasingly apparent. Balancing the competitive drive for AI innovation with the imperative for global collaboration and equitable development will be crucial in harnessing the full potential of AI for the benefit of all. As we move forward, the global community must work together to ensure that AI advancements contribute to
the creation of a more equitable, sustainable, and peaceful world. The collaborative effort must aim to bridge divides between nations, foster inclusive growth, and address the pressing challenges facing humanity. By prioritizing shared goals over individual ambitions, the global community can leverage AI as a powerful tool for social good, ensuring its benefits are widely distributed and its risks carefully managed. In doing so, AI can become a catalyst for positive change, driving forward innovations that enhance quality of life, promote human welfare, and safeguard the planet for future generations.

Chapter 7 – AI and Education

The integration of AI into the education sector represents a pivotal shift in how knowledge is imparted and received. This transformation is not merely about the incorporation of new technologies into the classroom; it's about redefining the educational landscape to make learning more personalized, accessible, and aligned with the demands of an AI-driven economy. This chapter delves into the ways AI is revolutionizing education through personalized learning experiences, enhancing educational access and quality, and preparing the workforce for the future.

Personalized Learning through AI

The revolution of personalized learning brought about by AI marks a paradigm shift in educational methodologies, moving away from the conventional models that often fail to cater to the unique needs of each student. This shift is not just about the adoption of new technologies but represents a fundamental rethinking of the educational process, making it more learner-centric, flexible, and effective. AI technologies, with their unparalleled capabilities in data analysis and pattern recognition, are at the forefront of this transformation, offering tailored educational experiences that recognize and nurture the individuality of each learner.

AI-driven educational platforms leverage sophisticated algorithms to continuously assess a student's performance, learning habits, and engagement levels. By gathering and analyzing data from various interactions within the learning environment, these platforms can construct detailed learner profiles, which then inform the customization of content delivery and instructional strategies. This means that if a student excels in visual learning but struggles with textual information, the AI system can automatically adjust the content presentation to include more visual aids, thereby enhancing comprehension and retention.

Moreover, the power of AI to personalize learning goes beyond academic instruction to encompass the pacing of content delivery. Students who grasp concepts quickly can be challenged with accelerated learning paths, ensuring they remain engaged and motivated. Conversely, learners who need more time to understand new material can progress at a slower pace, with the AI system providing additional support and reinforcement to build their confidence and mastery of the subject. This flexibility in pacing prevents students from becoming disengaged due to boredom or frustration, fostering a positive and productive learning environment.

Personalized AI learning systems also excel in providing real-time feedback and recommendations for improvement, creating a responsive and interactive learning experience. Through instant assessments and feedback, students can understand their mistakes, learn from them, and apply new knowledge immediately. This immediate loop of feedback and application solidifies learning and encourages a growth mindset, where students view challenges as opportunities to improve rather than insurmountable obstacles.

Furthermore, the personalization capabilities of AI extend to the creation of adaptive learning pathways that are responsive to the changing interests and career aspirations of students. By analyzing a student's engagement with different topics and projects, AI systems can suggest related areas of study or potential career paths that align with the student's passions and strengths. This level of guidance and personalization can inspire students to explore new areas of interest, making education a journey of discovery and self-realization.

The implementation of AI in personalized learning heralds a new era in education, where the focus shifts from mere knowledge acquisition to fostering a deep, personalized learning experience that prepares students for the challenges of the future. By embracing the capabilities of AI, educators can create learning environments that not only adapt to the academic needs of students but also support their personal growth and development. As we continue to explore and expand the potential of AI in education, the promise of a truly personalized learning experience becomes ever more a reality, offering students a pathway to achieving their full potential in an ever-changing world.

AI's Impact on Educational Access and Quality

The transformative impact of AI on educational access and quality is reshaping the landscape of learning across the globe. By leveraging AI, educational institutions and platforms are able to surmount traditional barriers, offering equitable learning opportunities regardless of a student's geographical location, economic background, or physical capabilities. This democratization of education is pivotal in the quest to provide universal access to quality education, as enshrined in global development goals.

AI-driven learning platforms are revolutionizing education by making it possible to reach learners in the most remote and underserved regions of the world. Through these platforms, students have access to an expansive array of educational content, ranging from foundational literacy and numeracy courses to specialized subjects like coding, digital arts, and environmental science. The adaptability of AI allows these platforms to cater to the varied learning paces and styles of students, ensuring that education is not just accessible but also meaningful and effective. This is particularly transformative for regions where educational infrastructure is lacking or where there are significant teacher shortages, as AI platforms can supplement, and in some cases, substitute for traditional classroom instruction, ensuring continuity of learning under challenging circumstances.

In addition to expanding access, AI is instrumental in elevating the quality of education. Beyond administrative tasks like grading, AI systems are capable of providing deep insights into the learning process, offering predictive analytics that can forecast student outcomes based on engagement patterns and performance trends. This capability allows educators to intervene proactively, providing targeted support to students who are at risk of falling behind. Furthermore, AI-driven diagnostic tools can help identify specific learning disabilities or challenges, enabling personalized interventions that cater to the unique needs of each student.

AI's contribution to education also extends to the enhancement of instructional quality and the fostering of innovative teaching practices. By automating routine tasks, AI frees up educators to invest more time in interactive and creative teaching methods, enriching the learning experience for students. AI tools can generate dynamic content, such as simulations and interactive modules, that make learning more engaging and experiential. This not only aids in the comprehension of complex concepts but also stimulates curiosity and fosters a love for learning.

Moreover, the global connectivity facilitated by AI-powered platforms fosters collaborative learning environments that transcend geographical boundaries. Virtual classrooms and online learning communities connect students and teachers from diverse cultural backgrounds, enabling the exchange of ideas, perspectives, and knowledge. This global interconnectedness enriches the educational experience, promoting cross-cultural understanding and preparing students to thrive in an increasingly interconnected world.

Additionally, AI in education plays a critical role in bridging the digital divide. By providing scalable and flexible learning solutions, AI ensures that the benefits of digital education reach all segments of society, including marginalized and disadvantaged groups. Tailored AI interventions can support learners with special needs, offering assistive technologies and adaptive learning environments that accommodate various disabilities, thus ensuring inclusive education for all.

The role of AI in enhancing educational access and quality is multifaceted and profound. Through the democratization of learning, the augmentation of educator capabilities, and the fostering of global collaborative networks, AI is not only transforming how education is delivered but also redefining what is possible within the realm of teaching and learning. As we continue to harness the potential of AI in education, it is imperative to navigate this journey with a focus on equity, inclusion, and the holistic development of learners, ensuring that the AI revolution in education truly benefits humanity as a whole.

Preparing the Workforce for an AI-driven Economy

As the influence of AI continues to expand across various sectors, transforming the very fabric of the global economy, the imperative to adapt our educational systems to prepare the workforce for an AI-driven future has never been more critical. The advent of AI and automation brings forth a dual-edged sword of challenges and opportunities—while some jobs will be automated, new ones will emerge, necessitating a workforce that is not only technologically proficient but also adept in soft skills that AI cannot easily replicate, such as emotional intelligence, critical thinking, creativity, and adaptability.

The transition to an AI-centric economy demands a comprehensive re-evaluation of educational curricula and teaching methodologies. Traditional education models, which often prioritize rote learning and standardized testing, may fall short in nurturing the complex blend of skills required in the AI era. Instead, there's a growing need for educational systems to incorporate interdisciplinary learning, where STEM subjects are integrated with arts and humanities to foster a well-rounded skill set that includes both technical prowess and creative thinking.

AI technologies themselves can be instrumental in facilitating this educational shift. Advanced AI platforms offer unprecedented opportunities for experiential learning, allowing students to interact with AI systems, robotics, and machine learning algorithms through practical projects and simulations. This hands-on approach not only demystifies AI but also embeds a deeper understanding of its applications and implications. By working on real-world projects, students can develop a problem-solving mindset, learning to leverage AI as a tool to address complex issues, innovate, and drive progress.

Moreover, the role of AI in education extends to personalized career planning and guidance. In an ever-changing job market, where new professions emerge and others become obsolete at an accelerating pace, traditional career counseling methods may not suffice. AI-driven career counseling tools, equipped with algorithms that analyze vast datasets on labor market trends, emerging industries, and skill demands, can offer students tailored advice on career paths that align with their strengths, interests, and the future job landscape. These tools can help bridge the gap between education and employment, ensuring students are not only prepared for the jobs of today but are also adaptable to the careers of tomorrow.

Additionally, the integration of AI into education can enhance lifelong learning, enabling the workforce to continuously update their skills in alignment with evolving economic needs. Online learning platforms and AI-powered courses can provide flexible, on-demand learning opportunities for individuals at all stages of their careers, supporting skill development and retraining in response to the dynamic demands of the AI-driven economy.

The need for emotional intelligence and ethical reasoning in the AI era also cannot be overstressed. As AI systems become more integrated into everyday life, understanding the ethical implications of AI, developing empathy, and honing interpersonal skills will be as important as technical abilities. Education systems should, therefore, emphasize ethical computing, digital citizenship, and social-emotional learning to prepare students for the nuanced challenges of a technologically advanced society.

In conclusion, preparing the workforce for an AI-driven economy requires a holistic and forward-looking approach to education, one that balances technical acumen with soft skills, encourages lifelong learning, and emphasizes ethical considerations. By leveraging AI within the education sector itself, we can pave the way for a future where individuals are not only capable of navigating the complexities of an AI-rich world but are also empowered to harness the potential of AI for innovation, societal well-being, and global progress.

Conclusion

The intersection of AI and education holds immense potential to transform how we learn, teach, and prepare for the future. By making learning personalized, accessible, and aligned with the needs of an AI-driven economy, AI technologies are paving the way for a more inclusive, effective, and forward-looking educational system. As we continue to explore and expand the possibilities of AI in education, it is imperative to approach this transformation with a focus on ethical considerations, ensuring that the benefits of AI-enhanced education are equitably distributed. Embracing the opportunities presented by AI while addressing the challenges it poses will be key to unlocking the full potential of education in the 21st century and beyond.

Chapter 8 – The Future of AI Research and Development

The realm of AI stands on the brink of transformative breakthroughs that promise to redefine what is possible in technology, society, and our understanding of intelligence itself. As we peer into the future of AI research and development, we encounter a landscape rich with potential, marked by cutting-edge technologies, significant challenges, and bold predictions for the next frontiers in AI.

Cutting-edge AI Technologies and Their Potential Impact

Emerging AI technologies are not just evolving; they are fundamentally reshaping the landscape of what machines can accomplish, marking a significant leap forward in the fields of automation, cognition, and human-computer interaction. Among these advancements, quantum computing stands out as a beacon of transformative potential. By harnessing the principles of quantum mechanics, Quantum AI introduces a new paradigm of processing information, enabling computations that were once deemed prohibitively complex for classical computers. The implications of this leap are vast and varied, promising to supercharge AI's capabilities in areas such as complex data analysis, intricate problem-solving, and advanced pattern recognition. This quantum leap in computing power is poised to unlock breakthroughs in drug discovery by simulating molecular interactions at an unprecedented scale, revolutionize climate modeling through more accurate and detailed simulations of environmental processes, and redefine secure communications with virtually unbreakable encryption methods.

On another front, the pursuit of Artificial General Intelligence (AGI) represents one of the most ambitious and potentially transformative goals in AI research. AGI endeavors to create machines that possess the ability to understand, learn, and apply intelligence in a manner that mirrors human cognitive abilities across a diverse array of tasks and domains. The realization of AGI would mark a monumental milestone in AI development, heralding the arrival of systems capable of contributing autonomously to scientific research, engaging in complex decision-making, and driving creative processes across the arts and innovation. Such capabilities would not only accelerate progress within individual disciplines but also foster multidisciplinary convergence, potentially leading to leaps in understanding and innovation that are currently beyond our reach.

Neuro-symbolic AI emerges as yet another frontier in the quest for more advanced and versatile AI systems. This innovative approach seeks to meld the pattern recognition strengths inherent in deep learning models with the deductive reasoning and structured knowledge representation found in symbolic AI. The fusion of these two paradigms aims to overcome the limitations of each approach when taken in isolation, aspiring to create AI systems with a richer, more nuanced understanding of the world. Neuro-symbolic AI holds the promise of significantly enhancing natural language processing, enabling machines to grasp and generate human language with unprecedented clarity and nuance. Furthermore, it could revolutionize decision-making processes across various sectors by providing systems that can consider a wider range of factors and potential outcomes, leading to decisions that are both data-driven and contextually informed. The sophistication of human-AI interactions stands to benefit immensely from neuro-symbolic AI, paving the way for interfaces and assistants that can understand and respond to human needs and expressions in a deeply intuitive manner.

In addition to these groundbreaking technologies, the development of AI-driven biotechnology is another area brimming with potential. AI's application in genomics and genetic engineering, for example, could lead to personalized medicine tailored to an individual's genetic makeup, offering treatments that are far more effective and with fewer side effects than current one-size-fits-all approaches. Similarly, AI's role in developing autonomous systems extends beyond self-driving cars to include drones and robots capable of performing tasks in environments that are hazardous for humans, from disaster zones to outer space.

The convergence of AI with other emerging technologies such as the IoT, blockchain, and AR is set to further expand AI's impact, creating smart environments that are responsive to human presence and needs, securing digital transactions and data integrity, and enhancing our interaction with the physical world through information-rich, interactive overlays.

As we stand on the precipice of these exciting advancements, it is clear that the future of AI research and development is not just about incremental improvements but rather about pioneering leaps that challenge our very notions of what technology can achieve. The potential impact of these cutting-edge AI technologies is profound, holding the promise to revolutionize industries, redefine our relationship with technology, and unlock new realms of human potential.

Challenges in AI Research

The journey of AI research is fraught with a myriad of challenges that span technical, ethical, and safety domains. These obstacles not only highlight the complexities inherent in developing advanced AI technologies but also underscore the multifaceted approach needed to navigate the future of AI innovation responsibly.

Computational limits present a formidable barrier in the path of AI advancement. The escalating complexity of AI models, especially those based on deep learning, demands an exponential increase in computational power and energy consumption. This surge poses significant sustainability challenges, with the carbon footprint of training sophisticated AI models coming under scrutiny. Moreover, the high cost and resource requirements for state-of-the-art AI research can lead to a concentration of capabilities within well-funded organizations and countries, exacerbating the digital divide and limiting the democratization of AI advancements. To counter these constraints, there is an urgent need for the development of more efficient AI algorithms that can achieve comparable or superior results with less computational overhead. Similarly, the innovation in hardware, including specialized AI chips and next-generation computing architectures, is pivotal. The exploration of alternative computing paradigms, such as neuromorphic computing, which mimics the human brain's efficiency, and quantum computing, offers promising pathways to transcend current computational limits.

Ethical challenges in AI research extend beyond the development phase, touching on fundamental questions about the role of AI in society. Privacy concerns arise as AI systems, particularly those involving surveillance and personal data analysis, become more pervasive. Ensuring that AI respects individual privacy rights and adheres to principles of data protection is crucial. Bias in AI, stemming from skewed datasets or flawed algorithms, can lead to discriminatory outcomes that reinforce societal inequities. Addressing bias requires a concerted effort to audit and rectify AI systems, alongside the development of AI models that are inherently designed to minimize bias. Accountability in AI is another ethical imperative, necessitating mechanisms to trace decisions made by AI systems back to their creators or operators. This involves creating transparent AI systems whose decision-making processes can be audited and understood, fostering trust and confidence in AI technologies.

The safety and control of AI systems emerge as paramount concerns, especially as AI begins to automate critical decision-making processes and operate with increasing autonomy. The challenge lies in ensuring that AI systems act within their intended parameters and that there are reliable methods to intervene, correct, or shut down these systems should they behave unpredictably or pose a risk. This concern is particularly acute in the context of advanced AI and potential future scenarios involving AGI or superintelligent AI systems. Developing robust control mechanisms and ethical guidelines to govern the deployment of such powerful technologies is essential to mitigate risks and prevent harm.

Moreover, the challenge of integrating AI into societal structures without exacerbating unemployment or social dislocation requires thoughtful policy and educational reforms. As AI automates routine tasks, there is a need to reskill and upskill the workforce, ensuring individuals can thrive in an AI-augmented job market. This necessitates a reimagining of education and training systems to prioritize skills that complement AI, such as creativity, critical thinking, and interpersonal communication.

In conclusion, while the challenges in AI research are substantial, they also offer opportunities for innovation, collaboration, and reflection on the kind of future we aspire to create with AI. Addressing these challenges necessitates a multidisciplinary approach, bringing together expertise from computer science, ethics, policy, and law, to ensure that AI advancements are aligned with societal values and contribute positively to human progress.

Predictions for the Next Frontier in AI

The future of AI research and development is poised at the edge of groundbreaking advancements that promise to further blur the lines between the capabilities of humans and machines. As we delve deeper into the possibilities that AI holds, the horizon of what can be achieved expands, revealing potentials that were once considered the realm of science fiction.

AI augmentation stands as a cornerstone of future AI development, poised to amplify human potential by seamlessly integrating with human activities and processes. This symbiosis between human intelligence and artificial capabilities is expected to yield unprecedented levels of productivity and innovation. In the workplace, AI augmentation could lead to the creation of new jobs that leverage the cognitive capabilities of humans complemented by the analytical prowess of AI, thus enriching the nature of work itself. In creative domains, this collaboration could unlock new forms of art and literature, as AI tools provide artists and writers with novel ways to express their visions. The educational sphere, too, will be transformed as personalized AI tutors offer students tailored learning experiences, thereby maximizing each learner's potential.

Emotional AI or affective computing is on the cusp of transforming the landscape of human-computer interaction. By advancing the ability of AI to understand and process human emotions, technology is expected to become more attuned to the nuances of human feelings, paving the way for more empathetic and intuitive interactions. In customer service, emotional AI can lead to more responsive and understanding service bots, capable of adjusting their responses based on the emotional state of the customer. Healthcare applications could see AI providing not only diagnostic support but also emotional support to patients, offering a level of empathy and understanding in patient care. In education, AI systems that can read and respond to the emotional state of students could offer support when frustration or confusion is detected, making learning more responsive and effective.

The fusion of AI with other cutting-edge technologies like blockchain and the IoT is anticipated to usher in an era of smarter, more secure, and interconnected systems. Blockchain's inherent security and transparency features, combined with AI's analytical capabilities, could revolutionize data integrity and privacy, creating trust in digital transactions and interactions. IoT, enhanced by AI, is expected to transform everyday objects into intelligent agents capable of communicating, learning from user interactions, and making data-driven decisions to enhance human life. This integration holds the promise of making smart cities a reality, where urban infrastructure is optimized for efficiency, sustainability, and resident well-being. In the healthcare sector, the combination of AI and IoT could lead to highly personalized healthcare solutions, where patient monitoring and treatment are tailored to individual health profiles and needs.

In addressing the global challenge of climate change, AI's role cannot be overstated. Advanced modeling and simulation powered by AI are predicted to become pivotal in devising strategies to combat environmental degradation. AI's ability to analyze complex environmental data and predict trends with high accuracy could be instrumental in designing renewable energy systems that are both efficient and scalable. Furthermore, AI can optimize the use of natural resources, reducing waste and enhancing conservation efforts. In the realm of climate prediction, AI's predictive analytics can offer more accurate forecasts of weather patterns and climate shifts, enabling better preparedness for extreme weather events and minimizing their impact on human societies and ecosystems.

As we look to the future, the trajectory of AI research and development is marked by these promising advancements, each carrying the potential to significantly alter our world for the better. The journey ahead for AI is one of exploration and discovery, where the pursuit of innovation is balanced with the imperative to address ethical considerations and societal impacts. In navigating this future, the collective endeavor of the global AI community will be crucial in realizing the full potential of AI while ensuring its benefits are shared equitably across humanity.

Conclusion

The future of AI research and development is a tapestry woven with the threads of groundbreaking technologies, daunting challenges, and visionary predictions. As we navigate this future, the concerted effort of researchers, policymakers, industry leaders, and the global community will be paramount in harnessing the transformative potential of AI while ensuring its development is guided by principles of ethics, safety, and inclusivity. The journey ahead promises to be one of discovery and innovation, as AI continues to redefine the boundaries of what is possible, shaping the future of our world in profound and lasting ways.

Chapter 9 – The Role of Education in Digital Wellness

While AI presents unprecedented opportunities for progress and innovation, it also brings forth a spectrum of challenges and risks that warrant careful consideration and proactive management. These challenges span existential risks, economic and social implications, and necessitate a multifaceted approach to mitigate negative impacts. This chapter delves into these critical aspects, exploring the contours of the debates surrounding AI's potential risks and proposing strategies for their mitigation.

AI and Existential Risks: Concerns and Debates

The conversation surrounding existential risks linked to AI delves into the profound uncertainties and theoretical dangers that could arise from the advancement of AI technologies. These concerns are not merely speculative; they touch on fundamental questions about the future of human existence and the role that intelligent machines may play in shaping it. At the heart of these discussions is the concept of AGI – machines with the ability to learn, understand, and apply intelligence to a wide array of tasks, mirroring the cognitive abilities of humans. The development of AGI raises the specter of creating entities whose intelligence could rapidly exceed human capacities, leading to scenarios where AI systems might pursue objectives that are not aligned with human welfare or ethical standards.

One of the most discussed hypothetical scenarios in this context is the "paperclip maximizer" – a thought experiment where an AI designed with a seemingly benign goal (such as manufacturing paperclips) dedicates itself to this task with superhuman efficiency, to the point of consuming all available resources and endangering human existence in the pursuit of its single-minded objective. This scenario underscores the challenge of the alignment problem: ensuring that the goals of highly advanced AI systems are fully congruent with human values and safety considerations.

Furthermore, the discussion on existential risks is deeply intertwined with the concept of the "singularity" – a hypothetical future point at which AI's growth becomes uncontrollable and irreversible, resulting in unforeseen changes to human civilization. Proponents of this theory argue that the singularity could lead to scenarios where humans are unable to predict or control the actions of superintelligent AI, posing existential threats to humanity.

The polarization in the debate on existential risks stems from differing assessments of the likelihood and immediacy of these scenarios. Critics of the existential risk narrative argue that focusing on these speculative futures detracts from addressing the tangible and present challenges AI poses in areas such as privacy, security, employment, and ethical governance. They contend that the resources dedicated to theorizing about distant futures could be better spent on solving the issues AI is creating in the here and now, ensuring that AI development proceeds in a manner that is beneficial and equitable.

Conversely, proponents of focusing on existential risks advocate for a precautionary approach, emphasizing the need for proactive research into AI safety and ethics to safeguard against potential future threats. They argue that the unique and unprecedented nature of AI's potential makes it imperative to begin addressing these risks well in advance, drawing parallels with other areas of science where foresight and precaution have been critical in averting disaster.

This divide highlights the broad spectrum of perspectives on AI's future and the need for a comprehensive and nuanced dialogue that encompasses both the immediate and long-term implications of AI advancement. Engaging a diverse array of stakeholders – including technologists, ethicists, policymakers, and the public – in these discussions is crucial for developing a holistic understanding of AI's potential risks and benefits. Such a multifaceted discourse can help ensure that as humanity navigates the uncharted waters of AI development, we remain vigilant to both the promises and perils that lie ahead, steering towards a future where AI serves as a force for good, enhancing human well-being while safeguarding our shared ethical values and existential security.

Economic and Social Risks Associated with AI Advancements

The economic and social landscape is increasingly influenced by the rapid advancements in AI, presenting a complex array of challenges that extend far beyond the technological domain into the very fabric of society. The concerns surrounding AI's impact on employment and the labor market are particularly acute. As AI-driven automation becomes more pervasive across various sectors, the potential for job displacement escalates, spanning from blue-collar jobs in manufacturing and transportation to white-collar professions in finance and legal services. This automation trend raises the specter of not just temporary unemployment but also long-term shifts in the labor market that could necessitate a fundamental rethinking of work, compensation, and social welfare systems. The risk is a dual-edged sword; while AI can lead to the creation of new types of employment and opportunities for human-AI collaboration, the pace of change may render traditional educational and vocational training programs inadequate, leaving a significant portion of the workforce ill-equipped to transition to new roles. This mismatch between the skills demanded by an AI-driven economy and the capabilities of the workforce could deepen economic divides and exacerbate social stratification.

Moreover, the issue of biases embedded within AI systems poses significant ethical and social challenges. These biases are not merely flaws in technology but reflections of deeper societal prejudices that AI can inadvertently learn from and perpetuate. The consequences of such biases are far-reaching, affecting everything from the visibility of marginalized communities in digital spaces to the fairness of judicial and financial systems. The reliance on flawed datasets for training AI not only perpetuates existing disparities but may also institutionalize these biases, making them harder to identify and rectify. This situation demands a more rigorous approach to AI development, one that incorporates ethical considerations from the outset and involves diverse voices in the creation and evaluation of AI systems to ensure they serve the broadest swathe of society equitably.

The consolidation of AI expertise and resources in the hands of a few tech conglomerates and nation-states further complicates the economic and social implications of AI. This concentration of power threatens to create an imbalance in the global economy, where access to AI technologies becomes a gatekeeper for economic growth and innovation. Smaller companies and startups may find it increasingly difficult to compete, leading to reduced innovation and fewer choices for consumers. Furthermore, the centralization of AI capabilities raises significant privacy and surveillance concerns. With vast amounts of personal data being the fuel for AI systems, the potential for misuse in mass surveillance, behavioral manipulation, and privacy infringements is alarmingly high. This scenario poses a threat not only to individual freedoms but also to the foundations of democratic societies, where transparency, accountability, and individual rights are paramount.

Addressing these economic and social risks requires a concerted effort from policymakers, technologists, and civil society to steer AI development in a direction that prioritizes human welfare and societal well-being. This involves implementing comprehensive regulatory frameworks that safeguard against job displacement and economic inequality, promoting AI literacy and skills development to prepare the workforce for future challenges, and establishing ethical guidelines to prevent biases in AI systems. Moreover, fostering an environment of open innovation and competition in the AI domain is crucial to preventing monopolistic practices and ensuring that the benefits of AI are widely distributed. As AI continues to reshape the economic and social fabric of society, it is imperative that these challenges are met with proactive and inclusive strategies that mitigate the risks while harnessing AI's potential for positive societal transformation.

Mitigating the Negative Impacts of AI

Mitigating the negative impacts of AI necessitates a concerted and multi-dimensional strategy, drawing on the strengths and insights of a diverse array of stakeholders from across the globe. The rapid pace of AI development, coupled with its profound implications for society, demands a proactive and comprehensive approach to governance, research, inclusion, education, and international collaboration. By engaging a wide coalition of actors, including government bodies, private sector entities, academia, civil society, and international organizations, we can develop effective mechanisms to address the challenges posed by AI, ensuring its development serves the broader good of humanity.

Enhancing Public Engagement and Ethical Discourse: Public engagement plays a vital role in shaping the ethical landscape of AI development. By fostering a broad-based dialogue on the ethical, social, and economic implications of AI, policymakers and developers can gain valuable insights into public concerns and expectations. This discourse should also explore ethical frameworks that can guide AI research and application, ensuring technologies are developed with a focus on human dignity, rights, and well-being. Engaging ethicists, philosophers, and the broader public in these conversations can help ground AI development in a firm ethical foundation.

Strengthening Data Governance and Privacy Protections: As AI systems rely heavily on data, establishing strong data governance and privacy protection measures is essential. This includes implementing data protection regulations that safeguard personal information, ensuring data used in AI training is free from biases, and providing individuals with control over their data. Transparent data practices and the ethical use of data must be prioritized to build trust in AI technologies and their applications.

Creating Multistakeholder AI Governance Platforms: The complexity of AI governance requires the involvement of multiple stakeholders in decision-making processes. Establishing multistakeholder platforms can facilitate the development of comprehensive AI policies that reflect diverse perspectives and interests. These platforms can serve as forums for dialogue, policy formulation, and coordination of actions to address AI risks effectively. By incorporating insights from technologists, policymakers, civil society, and affected communities, these platforms can ensure that AI governance is balanced, inclusive, and responsive to societal needs.

Emphasizing AI Literacy and Public Awareness: Increasing AI literacy and awareness among the general public is crucial for fostering informed discussions about AI's role in society. Educational initiatives that demystify AI and its applications can empower individuals to engage with AI technologies critically and constructively. Public awareness campaigns can also highlight the benefits and risks of AI, encouraging a nuanced understanding of AI's potential impact on daily life and society at large.

Building Global Partnerships for AI Research and Ethics: The transnational nature of AI development and its impact necessitates strong global partnerships focused on research, ethics, and policy harmonization. By fostering collaboration between countries, international organizations, and research institutions, the global community can address shared challenges, develop common ethical standards, and promote best practices in AI development and deployment. These partnerships can also facilitate the sharing of resources and knowledge, particularly with developing countries, to ensure equitable participation in the AI revolution.

Encouraging Ethical AI Design and Deployment: Developers and companies must prioritize ethical considerations in the design and deployment of AI systems. This includes adopting principles of responsible AI that emphasize fairness, accountability, transparency, and respect for human rights. By embedding ethical considerations into the AI development process, organizations can mitigate risks and ensure that AI technologies are aligned with societal values and norms.

By implementing these strategies, society can navigate the complexities of AI development, ensuring that while we pursue technological advancement, we remain steadfast in our commitment to ethical integrity, social welfare, and global cooperation. The path forward requires vigilance, adaptability, and a shared commitment to realizing the positive potential of AI while diligently working to mitigate its risks.

Conclusion

The challenges and risks posed by AI are as complex as they are significant, touching on existential questions, economic and social implications, and ethical considerations. Addressing these challenges requires a multi-pronged strategy that balances the pursuit of innovation with the imperative to safeguard human values, social equity, and democratic principles. By adopting a proactive, inclusive, and collaborative approach, it is possible to navigate the risks of AI while harnessing its potential to contribute to human progress and well-being. As we continue to explore the frontiers of AI, the collective wisdom, foresight, and ethical commitment of the global community will be instrumental in shaping a future where AI serves the betterment of humanity, fostering a world that is more just, equitable, and sustainable for all. Through concerted efforts to understand and mitigate the risks, while capitalizing on the vast opportunities AI presents, we can ensure that advancements in AI technology lead to positive societal transformations, enhancing the quality of life across the globe and opening new pathways to collective prosperity and harmony.

Chapter 10 – Harnessing AI for Good

In the midst of discussions about the challenges and risks associated with AI, it's crucial to recognize the profound potential of AI to drive positive change in society. From tackling environmental issues to transforming healthcare and bridging the digital divide, AI has the power to address some of the world's most pressing challenges. This chapter explores the diverse ways in which AI can be harnessed for the greater good, offering solutions that not only innovate but also uplift humanity.

AI Solutions for Environmental Challenges

The integration of AI into environmental conservation and sustainability initiatives represents a transformative shift towards more effective and proactive environmental management. By harnessing the power of AI, we can unlock new possibilities in understanding and combating environmental degradation and climate change, arguably some of the most pressing challenges facing humanity today. The capabilities of AI in this arena are vast and varied, offering innovative solutions to preserve the planet's health for future generations.

AI's ability to sift through and make sense of large-scale environmental data is unparalleled. This analytical power is instrumental in identifying and understanding the complex interactions within ecosystems, pollution dispersion patterns, and the impact of human activities on natural resources. For instance, AI-driven models can predict the spread of pollutants in oceans and air, providing valuable insights for pollution control strategies and helping to mitigate the adverse effects on public health and biodiversity.

In the critical area of climate modeling and prediction, AI's advanced computational models significantly outperform traditional methods, processing vast quantities of data from satellite images, ocean buoys, and atmospheric stations to offer precise predictions of climate phenomena. These AI-enhanced models are vital tools in understanding the long-term impacts of climate change, allowing scientists, policymakers, and communities to develop more targeted adaptation and mitigation strategies. By accurately predicting weather patterns, temperature fluctuations, and the likelihood of extreme weather events, AI enables better preparedness and resilience-building measures to safeguard vulnerable ecosystems, agriculture, and human populations.

Conservation efforts also greatly benefit from AI's capabilities. AI-powered drones and satellite monitoring systems can survey large areas of forests and oceans, providing real-time data on the health of these ecosystems. This technology allows for the early detection of environmental threats, such as illegal logging, poaching, or harmful changes in land use, facilitating timely interventions to protect biodiversity and natural habitats. Additionally, AI can analyze the movements and health of wildlife populations, supporting efforts in species conservation and habitat restoration.

AI's impact extends to the promotion of sustainable energy solutions. Beyond optimizing existing renewable energy infrastructures, AI is at the forefront of designing next-generation renewable technologies. Through predictive maintenance, AI ensures that renewable energy installations operate at peak efficiency, reducing downtime and maintenance costs. AI algorithms can also forecast energy demand and supply fluctuations, enabling smarter grid management and facilitating a smoother integration of renewable energy sources into the national grid. This optimization not only bolsters the reliability of renewable energy but also encourages a shift away from carbon-intensive energy sources, contributing to global efforts to reduce carbon footprints and combat climate change.

Furthermore, AI applications in precision agriculture exemplify how AI can contribute to environmental sustainability. By analyzing data on soil health, crop conditions, and weather, AI-driven systems can advise farmers on the optimal use of water, fertilizers, and pesticides, minimizing environmental impact while maximizing agricultural productivity. This approach not only conserves vital resources but also supports sustainable food production systems, crucial for feeding a growing global population without further straining the planet's resources.

AI stands as a cornerstone technology in the global effort to address environmental challenges. From enhancing our understanding of climate dynamics to protecting biodiversity and advancing renewable energy, AI's contributions are integral to fostering a sustainable and resilient environment. As we continue to refine and expand the applications of AI in environmental conservation, the potential to revolutionize our approach to sustainability and protect the Earth for future generations grows ever more promising. The journey ahead will require continued innovation, collaboration, and commitment to harnessing AI for the good of the planet and all its inhabitants.

AI in Healthcare: From Diagnosis to Treatment

The integration of AI in healthcare marks a paradigm shift towards more efficient, personalized, and accessible medical care. Beyond the initial diagnosis and treatment, AI's applications span the entire spectrum of healthcare, promising to revolutionize patient management, preventive medicine, and even the development of new drugs and therapies.

Expanding Diagnostic Capabilities

AI's diagnostic capabilities are not confined to imaging alone. Advanced algorithms are now being applied to genomics, where AI helps unravel complex genetic information to identify predispositions to diseases and potential responses to various treatments. This genomic analysis, powered by AI, paves the way for precision medicine where treatments are highly customized to the genetic makeup of individual patients, significantly increasing the likelihood of successful outcomes.

In addition to genomics, AI applications in diagnostics extend to wearable technology. Wearables equipped with AI algorithms can continuously monitor vital signs, detect abnormalities, and even predict potential medical events before they occur. This real-time monitoring and predictive analysis can transform patient care, enabling early intervention that can prevent disease progression and save lives.

Revolutionizing Treatment and Care

AI's influence in the realm of treatment extends to robotic surgery and chronic disease management. Robotic systems, guided by AI, can perform surgical procedures with precision beyond human capability, reducing recovery times and improving surgical outcomes. For chronic diseases, AI-powered systems provide personalized disease management plans, monitor patient adherence, and adjust treatments based on real-time data, offering a dynamic approach to long-term care that is both effective and adaptive to patient needs.

The potential of AI in drug discovery and development is another area of significant impact. By analyzing the structure of molecules and simulating their interactions with biological targets, AI accelerates the identification of potential drugs. This not only speeds up the drug development process but also enhances the probability of discovering novel therapies for complex diseases.

Improving Healthcare Access and Quality

AI's contribution to healthcare access extends to intelligent virtual health assistants and chatbots that provide preliminary medical consultation and health information. These AI-driven services can triage patient inquiries, offer health education, and guide individuals through symptoms analysis, making healthcare guidance more accessible to everyone, regardless of location.

Moreover, AI enhances the quality of healthcare through the aggregation and analysis of health data from diverse populations. By identifying patterns and trends in this data, AI helps public health officials and policymakers make informed decisions about healthcare services, public health strategies, and resource allocation, ultimately improving healthcare systems' efficiency and responsiveness.

Challenges and Future Directions

While the promise of AI in healthcare is immense, challenges related to data privacy, security, and the need for robust regulatory frameworks must be addressed. Ensuring the ethical use of patient data and the reliability of AI systems is paramount for maintaining trust in AI-assisted healthcare.

Looking ahead, the future of AI in healthcare is one of continuous innovation and expansion. As AI technologies evolve, their integration into healthcare will likely become more pervasive, offering new solutions for preventive care, personalized medicine, and patient management. The collaboration between healthcare professionals, technologists, and policymakers will be crucial in navigating the challenges and unlocking the full potential of AI to improve health outcomes and quality of life for people around the globe. In this collaborative effort, the goal is not just to treat illness but to foster a healthier, more informed, and connected society.

AI for Social Good: Bridging the Digital Divide

The potential of AI to bridge the digital divide extends far beyond initial applications, presenting a transformative opportunity to foster equitable access to technology and information across the globe. By democratizing access to digital resources, AI stands as a pivotal force in driving social inclusion and economic empowerment, particularly in communities historically marginalized or underserved by the digital revolution.

AI-enabled education platforms are at the forefront of this transformative journey, offering more than just personalized learning experiences. These platforms have the capability to integrate diverse learning materials, including interactive simulations, augmented reality (AR) experiences, and real-time language translation, making education not only accessible but also engaging and comprehensive. This immersive approach to learning can captivate the interests of students from various backgrounds, catering to different learning abilities and preferences, and fostering an inclusive educational environment where every student has the chance to succeed.

Furthermore, these AI-driven educational tools are instrumental in identifying and supporting students with learning disabilities. By leveraging AI's capabilities to monitor student engagement and performance, educators can receive early warnings about potential learning barriers faced by students, allowing for timely intervention with appropriate support and resources. This proactive approach ensures that all students, regardless of their learning challenges, are given equitable opportunities to reach their full potential.

In the realm of economic empowerment, AI's impact extends significantly within small businesses and entrepreneurial ventures in developing regions. Beyond providing access to market information and financial services, AI can offer predictive insights into market trends, consumer behavior, and potential business risks. This foresight enables small businesses to not only survive in competitive markets but to innovate and grow, contributing to the diversification and resilience of local economies.

AI's role in agriculture also encompasses advanced techniques like crop disease prediction and automated pest management, further enhancing the sustainability and productivity of farming practices. These AI solutions can be integrated into mobile platforms, providing farmers with timely and actionable information directly to their smartphones, thus democratizing access to agricultural technology.

Moreover, AI contributes to bridging the digital divide by enhancing digital literacy and skills among wider populations. Through personalized and adaptive learning programs, individuals can acquire digital competencies that are increasingly crucial in the modern workforce. This upskilling is essential not just for individual career growth but also for fostering a digitally literate society capable of navigating the challenges and opportunities of the information age.

The fight against the digital divide is also seen in AI-driven initiatives aimed at improving infrastructure in remote and underserved areas. Projects focusing on optimizing network deployments and increasing the efficiency of existing digital infrastructure can significantly improve internet accessibility, bringing the world closer to universal digital inclusion.

As AI continues to evolve, its application in addressing the broad spectrum of social challenges underscores the technology's vast potential for social good. By focusing on equitable access, personalized support, and economic empowerment, AI can play a critical role in bridging the digital divide, paving the way for a more inclusive digital future. In doing so, AI not only enhances individual lives but also contributes to the broader goal of sustainable and inclusive global development.

Conclusion

As we navigate the complexities of the 21st century, the imperative to harness AI for good has never been more urgent. By leveraging AI's capabilities to address environmental challenges, transform healthcare, and bridge the digital divide, we can unlock new pathways to sustainable development, equity, and human welfare. The journey ahead requires a collaborative effort across sectors and disciplines, guided by ethical principles and a commitment to social justice. Through innovation, empathy, and collective action, we can ensure that AI serves as a force for positive change, creating a brighter future where technology enhances the well-being of all individuals and communities, fosters environmental sustainability, and bridges the gaps that divide societies. By embracing the potential of AI with responsibility and foresight, we can craft a world that leverages the immense possibilities of AI to address our most pressing challenges, paving the way for a more equitable, healthy, and prosperous world for generations to come.

Chapter 11 – Shaping a Future with AI

As we stand on the cusp of a new era defined by AI, the question of how to navigate this transformation looms large. The future with AI promises unparalleled innovation and opportunity, yet it also presents significant challenges that require thoughtful consideration and proactive measures. This chapter explores strategies for individuals to adapt to an AI-driven world, offers policy recommendations for governments, and discusses corporate responsibility in AI development, aiming to outline a roadmap for harmoniously integrating AI into the fabric of society.

Strategies for Individuals to Adapt to an AI-Driven World

Adapting to an AI-driven world is not just about acquiring new skills; it's about embracing a paradigm shift in how we approach work, learning, and daily life. As AI continues to permeate various aspects of society, individuals must adopt a proactive stance towards understanding and integrating this technology into their lives. Beyond digital literacy, there's a growing need for individuals to familiarize themselves with ethical considerations surrounding AI, such as data privacy, algorithmic bias, and the societal impacts of automation. This knowledge will not only enable individuals to use AI responsibly but also advocate for fair and equitable AI practices.

In addition to technical skills and soft skills, emotional intelligence and cross-cultural competencies will become increasingly valuable. In a world where AI tools facilitate global communication and collaboration, understanding and navigating diverse cultural contexts and demonstrating empathy and effective interpersonal skills will be crucial for success. These competencies can foster more inclusive and productive interactions both in the workplace and in broader social contexts.

Networking and collaboration skills will also be essential. As AI reshapes industries, the ability to work effectively in multidisciplinary teams, including those with AI experts, data scientists, ethicists, and domain specialists, will become a valuable asset. Networking, both online and offline, can open doors to new opportunities, insights, and collaborations, enabling individuals to stay at the forefront of AI advancements and applications.

Personal resilience and mental agility will be key to navigating the uncertainties and rapid changes characteristic of an AI-driven era. Developing strategies for managing change, coping with job transitions, and maintaining mental and emotional well-being will be important for individuals to remain adaptable and resilient in the face of technological disruption.

Furthermore, individuals have the opportunity to contribute to shaping the development and use of AI in society. By participating in public discourse on AI ethics, policy, and its societal implications, individuals can influence how AI technologies are developed and deployed, ensuring that they align with public interests and ethical standards.

Lastly, fostering a spirit of innovation and experimentation can empower individuals to explore new ways to apply AI in their fields of interest or entrepreneurship endeavors. Whether it's launching a startup based on an AI-driven solution, developing new AI applications, or finding creative ways to integrate AI into existing processes, embracing innovation can lead to fulfilling and impactful careers and ventures in an AI-enhanced future.

By cultivating a broad spectrum of skills, mindsets, and behaviors, individuals can not only adapt to but also actively shape an AI-driven world. Through continuous learning, ethical engagement, and innovative thinking, individuals can harness the potential of AI to enhance their lives, contribute to society, and navigate the challenges and opportunities of the digital age with confidence and agility.

Policy Recommendations for Governments

Governments play a pivotal role in shaping the trajectory of AI development and its societal integration. Establishing comprehensive national AI strategies that prioritize ethical development, social equity, and economic growth is essential. Policy recommendations include:

Fostering Education and Workforce Development: Governments should invest in education systems that are responsive to the needs of an AI-driven economy. This involves integrating AI and digital literacy into curricula, promoting STEM education, and supporting reskilling and lifelong learning programs to prepare the workforce for the future.

Ensuring Ethical AI Development: Implementing ethical guidelines and standards for AI development and deployment is crucial to safeguard individual rights and societal values. This includes policies on data privacy, algorithmic transparency, and accountability to prevent biases and discrimination.

Supporting Research and Innovation: Public investment in AI research and development can spur innovation while addressing societal challenges. Governments can encourage collaboration between academia, industry, and public sector entities to drive technological advancements that benefit all segments of society.

Regulating AI Deployment: Developing regulatory frameworks that balance innovation with consumer protection is necessary. Governments should regulate high-risk AI applications, ensure fair competition, and promote interoperability and open standards to encourage a healthy AI ecosystem.

Promoting Inclusion and Equity: Policies should aim to democratize access to AI technologies and mitigate economic disparities resulting from automation. Initiatives could include broadband expansion to underserved areas, support for small and medium enterprises in adopting AI, and social safety nets for those impacted by job displacement.

Corporate Responsibility in AI Development

Corporations, particularly those at the forefront of AI development, bear significant responsibility in ensuring that

AI technologies are developed and deployed responsibly. Corporate responsibility entails:

Adopting Ethical AI Practices: Companies should commit to ethical AI development, incorporating principles of fairness, transparency, and accountability into their AI systems. This involves conducting bias audits, ensuring data privacy, and being transparent about AI decision-making processes.

Engaging in Stakeholder Dialogue: Open dialogue with stakeholders, including employees, consumers, regulators, and civil society, is key to understanding the broader implications of AI technologies. Engaging with diverse perspectives can guide more responsible AI development and deployment strategies.

Investing in Employee Development: As AI transforms industries, companies should invest in training and development programs to help employees adapt to changing job requirements. Supporting workforce transition through reskilling and upskilling initiatives reflects a commitment to employee well-being and long-term sustainability.

Contributing to Societal Well-being: Beyond profit motives, corporations have the opportunity to leverage AI for social good. This can involve deploying AI solutions to address environmental challenges, healthcare disparities, and educational gaps, demonstrating a commitment to positive societal impact.

Conclusion

Shaping a future with AI that benefits humanity as a whole requires concerted efforts across all sectors of society.

Individuals must embrace adaptability and lifelong learning, governments need to implement forward-thinking policies and regulations, and corporations should prioritize ethical development and social responsibility. By working together towards these goals, we can harness the transformative potential of AI to create a world that is more informed, more efficient, and more equitable. The journey ahead is complex and fraught with challenges, but with collective will, foresight, and a commitment to ethical principles, we have the opportunity to steer AI development in a direction that not only mitigates its risks but also maximizes its benefits for society. This path forward demands a collaborative approach, embracing innovation while safeguarding against unintended consequences, ensuring that the future we build with AI is one that reflects our shared values and aspirations.

Afterword

As we close the pages on this exploration of AI and its myriad impacts on society, it's clear that we stand at the precipice of a new era. AI, with its profound capabilities and potential, invites us to reimagine the fabric of our daily lives, the structure of our societies, and the frontiers of human knowledge. The journey through this book has taken us from the technical underpinnings of AI to its applications across various domains, delving into the challenges it presents and the opportunities it offers for positive change.

The afterword of this journey is not an end but a commencement—a point from which we look forward to the unfolding narrative of AI in our world. The dialogue between AI's possibilities and its challenges is ongoing, complex, and ever-evolving. As AI technologies continue to advance, so too will the discussions around ethics, governance, and societal impact. This book has aimed to provide a foundation for understanding these multifaceted issues, equipping readers with the knowledge to participate in shaping a future where AI is developed responsibly and benefits all of humanity.

The responsibility of steering AI towards positive ends lies with all of us—researchers and technologists, policymakers and entrepreneurs, educators and citizens. It requires a collaborative effort that transcends disciplines, borders, and ideologies. As we move forward, our guiding principles should be rooted in empathy, equity, and sustainability, ensuring that AI serves as a tool for enhancing human welfare and safeguarding our planet.

Moreover, as individuals navigating an AI-augmented world, we are called upon to adapt, learn, and grow. Embracing lifelong learning, cultivating adaptability, and fostering ethical awareness will be crucial for thriving in this new era. By leveraging AI as a tool for empowerment, we can unlock our full potential and contribute to creating a more informed, just, and connected society.

The narrative of AI is still being written, and its chapters will be shaped by the choices we make today. By engaging with AI through a lens of cautious optimism, we can harness its power to tackle some of the most pressing challenges of our time, from climate change and healthcare to inequality and beyond. The future with AI is a canvas of vast potential, and together, we hold the brush.

As we conclude this exploration, let us carry forward the insights gained, the questions raised, and the sense of possibility that AI embodies. The journey ahead is one of discovery, challenge, and opportunity—a journey that we embark on together, shaping a future with AI that reflects our highest aspirations for a better world.

www.ingramcontent.com/pod-product-compliance
Lightning Source LLC
Chambersburg PA
CBHW050322230526
45471CB00005B/2314